CHAMPIONS OF FREEDOM

The Ludwig von Mises Lecture Series

CHAMPIONS OF FREEDOM

Volume 41

The Federal Income Tax
A Centenary Consideration

Gary Wolfram, Editor

Hillsdale College Press
Hillsdale, Michigan 49242

Hillsdale College Press

CHAMPIONS OF FREEDOM
The Ludwig von Mises Lecture Series—Volume 41
The Federal Income Tax: A Centenary Consideration

©2014 Hillsdale College Press, Hillsdale, Michigan 49242

First printing 2014

Printed in the United States of America

Front cover: © C.J. Burton/Corbis

Library of Congress Control Number: 2014937363

ISBN 978-0-916308-47-6

Contents

Contributors

W. Elliot Brownlee is Research Professor of history at the University of California, Santa Barbara. A graduate of Harvard University, he received his Ph.D. from the University of Wisconsin. He has held visiting appointments at Princeton University, Pepperdine University, the University of Tokyo, and Yokohama National University. Dr. Brownlee is the co-editor of *The Reagan Presidency: Pragmatic Conservatism and Its Legacies* and the author of *Federal Taxation in America: A Short History* and *Funding the Modern American State: The Rise and Fall of the Era of Easy Finance, 1941–1995.*

Kendrick A. Clements is a distinguished professor of history, emeritus, at the University of South Carolina. He received his M.A. and his Ph.D. in history from the University of California at Berkeley. He has published numerous articles in professional journals such as *Presidential Studies Quarterly* and *American Historical Review.* In addition, he is the editor of *James F. Byrnes and the Origins of the Cold War*, co-author of *Woodrow Wilson* (American Presidents Reference Series), and author of *William Jennings Bryan, Missionary Isolationist*; *Woodrow Wilson: World Statesman*; *The Presidency of Woodrow Wilson*; *Hoover, Conservation, and Consumerism: Engineering the Good Life*; and, most recently, *The Life of Herbert Hoover: Imperfect Visionary, 1918–1928.*

George Gilder is chairman of Gilder Publishing, LLC, editor-in-chief of *Gilder Technology Report*, and a senior fellow at the Discovery Institute. He pioneered the formulation of supply-side economics when he served as chairman of the Lehrman Institute's Economic Roundtable, and as a frequent contributor to Arthur B. Laffer's economic reports and *The Wall Street Journal*. He received the White House Award for Entrepreneurial Excellence from President Reagan in 1986. He is a contributing editor of *Forbes* and writes frequently for several publications, including *The Economist* and *American Spectator*. He is the author of several books, including *Men and Marriage, Wealth and Poverty*, and most recently, *Knowledge and Power.*

John E. Linder served as a U.S. Representative for the State of Georgia from 1993 to 2011. Prior to joining Congress, he was educated at the University of Minnesota and served in the United States Air Force. From 1996–1998, he joined the Republican Party leadership as Chairman of the National Republican Congressional Committee. Representative Linder sponsored the Fair Tax Act, first introducing the legislation in July 1999, and reintroducing it in every subsequent Congress. He is the co-author of *The FairTax Book*.

Daniel J. Mitchell is a senior fellow at the Cato Institute in Washington, D.C. Dr. Mitchell received his M.A. from the University of Georgia and his Ph.D. in economics from George Mason University. He has worked for the Heritage Foundation, former U.S. Senator Bob Packwood, and Citizens for a Sound Economy. He has written for several publications, including *The Wall Street Journal*, the *New York Times*, the *Washington Times*, *National Review*, *Forbes*, and *Investor's Business Daily*. He is the author of *The Flat Tax: Freedom, Fairness, Jobs, and Growth*.

Amity Shlaes is a syndicated columnist for *Bloomberg*, a director of the Four Percent Growth Project at the George W. Bush Presidential Center, and a member of the board of the Calvin Coolidge Memorial Foundation. She has served as a member of the editorial board of *The Wall Street Journal* and as a columnist for the *Financial Times*, and is a recipient of the Hayek Prize and the Frederic Bastiat Prize for free-market journalism. She is the author of four books, *Germany: The Empire Within*, *The Forgotten Man: A New History of the Great Depression*, *The Greedy Hand: How Taxes Drive Americans Crazy and What to Do About It*, and *Coolidge*.

Introduction

The 2013 Ludwig von Mises lecture series appropriately marked the 100th anniversary of the Sixteenth Amendment, which allowed for the enactment of the federal income tax. Federal government spending in 1913 was $715 million, less than 2 percent of U.S. gross domestic product. Last year, federal government expenditure was $3.712 trillion, which was 23.2 percent of gross domestic product. Federal government spending is thus not only massively larger in nominal terms, but is more than ten times larger relative to the size of the economy than it was in 1913.

There are a number of explanations for the massive growth in the federal government over the last one hundred years, but surely one of these is the ability of the federal government to raise revenue. A federal government limited to revenue from tariffs and excise taxes would not be able to fund massive entitlement programs such as Social Security and Medicare, regardless of the political circumstances.

In fiscal year 2013, taxes on income will account for nearly nine out of every ten dollars of receipts to the federal government. The personal income tax at $1.234 trillion accounts for 46 percent of receipts, and without the enactment of the Sixteenth Amendment the corporate income tax and the payroll taxes that generate an additional $1.3 trillion would not be constitutional. If our federal government was confined to excise taxes and custom duties, which were available to the federal government at the time of the Constitution, it would have receipts of $119 billion in fiscal year 2013. Today it is hard to imagine a federal government thus constrained.

With the advent of the income tax, the necessity of making the case for limited constitutional government became stronger. With a vast source of revenue available, the philosophical and theoretical arguments for the market economy and limited government that Ludwig von Mises put forth become crucial to defending liberty.

It is easy to imagine Mises giving one of the lectures on this topic. He emphasized that once government begins to intervene in the economy, it will create unintended consequences that will lead to further government intervention until the economy has moved inexorably toward central planning. The income tax began as a minor addition to the revenue of the federal government but it eventually enabled the intervention of the federal government to move along the path as Mises warned it would.

Another issue regarding the income tax is whether there are other tax structures that will provide us with more economic freedom and will lead to more efficient use of resources. The income tax allows government to interfere with economic activity through the use of deductions and credits. If the government wishes us to undertake some behavior that we would not normally choose to engage in, it will give us an income tax credit for doing so. It can thus use tax policy to extend the central planning that Mises warned against.

The income tax also reduces economic growth by taxing investment in capital—the machinery, buildings, data centers, and other goods that will make us more productive. This leads to another argument as to why the tax should be limited and perhaps replaced.

The essays in this volume, and the lectures from which they were taken, provide a history of the income tax, with the perspective of its effect on the growth of the federal government, as well as an analysis of the economic effects of the tax and suggestions for alternative methods of raising revenue.

Kendrick Clements approaches the income tax from a historical perspective, focusing on Woodrow Wilson in his essay, "Woodrow Wilson, Progressivism, and the Sixteenth Amendment." Clements provides a detailed discussion of the early history of the income tax and what led to the passage of the Sixteenth Amendment. He describes Wilson's reversal of position on the income tax, opposing it in 1906, privately supporting it as governor of New Jersey in 1910, and publicly supporting it in 1911.

Wilson was focused on reducing tariffs. This would lead to an improvement in the standard of living as imported products would compete against those produced by the large corporations of the time. The tariff bill led to a side issue of investigating the lobbying efforts of the trusts. The result of the investigation was not a finding of massive lobbying efforts by corporations, since they were so efficient by 1913 that they were unafraid of foreign competition, but rather a finding of large holdings by many senators in industries that would benefit from protectionism.

Clements describes the development of Wilson's thought as he came to believe the income tax was a fair way to raise the revenue necessary to prepare the nation for war and a useful social policy tool. He also discusses the developments in Congress that affected the form of the income tax, in particular its progressivity. Clements closes with an interesting statement, noting that while Wilson had presided over the beginnings of the modern income tax, it became a permanent fixture of peacetime government during the conservative Republican administrations that followed.

Amity Shlaes brings her knowledge of Warren Harding and Calvin Coolidge to bear on the problems of today in "Calvin Coolidge and the Moral Case for Economy." Harding won the presidency on a platform of normalcy, by which he meant slowing the incursion of Progressivism and returning to a predictable environment with smaller government, allowing business to thrive. Harding and his vice-president, Calvin Coolidge, were both very concerned with the federal budget.

Harding managed to cut the income tax rate from its World War I high, cajoled his department directors into cutting their budgets, and privatized the Naval Petroleum Reserves in an attempt to reduce the debt. Unfortunately, Harding's government became known for scandal, in particular the Teapot Dome Scandal, which cast a shadow over his presidency.

Upon Harding's sudden death in 1923, Calvin Coolidge became president. Shlaes details Coolidge's success at limiting the expenditures of the federal government. This in turn allowed him to reduce the income tax rate dramatically. Shlaes makes the interesting argument that Coolidge cut taxes not to spur economic growth, but to reduce government interference. Coolidge's stand on limiting government made him "enormously popular with voters." Her conclusion is that the best case for tax cuts is the moral case—bringing the federal government under control—and that we should be optimistic that this case can be made successfully today.

Elliot Brownlee, in "The Federal Income Tax: The First Hundred Years," provides a useful history of the tax, beginning with the enactment in 1861 of an income tax to raise revenue for the Civil War. Brownlee argues that the original intent of the income tax under President Wilson was to supplement weakening tariff revenues rather than finance a major expansion of the federal government. He also presents an interesting discussion of the debate over the progressivity of the tax and what "ability to pay" meant in the debates of the time. The 1916 Revenue Act transformed the tax into a mechanism for a redistribution of social power.

World War I and the expansion of the progressive income tax altered the political economy of taxation according to Brownlee. He offers a detailed analysis of the competing ideologies that developed with regard to how the income tax should be structured. Brownlee also covers the formation of the academic argument for what ought to be considered "income" with regard to both efficiency and equity.

Two other major national developments, the Great Depression and World War II, are discussed in terms of their effect on the income tax debate. Brownlee makes the insightful point that "every significant national crisis in American history—war (the Revolution, the Civil War, the two world wars) and the Great Depression—has been accompanied by new tax regimes." He discusses the effects these events had on both the political process and the practical application of the tax.

In the final portion of his essay, Brownlee divides the history of the income tax into three eras: the passage of the Sixteenth Amendment to World War II, from World War II to the 1970s and early 1980s, and the period that began with the passage of the Economic

Recovery Act of 1981. He examines the economic circumstances and the political process in each era. He closes with reasonable hope that the adoption of tax reform that focuses on the broadening of the tax base—which would reduce the economic inefficiencies associated with government's use of the tax code to affect our behavior—will eventually be possible.

George Gilder emphasizes the importance of information theory in "The Supply Side Insight." Gilder explains that the key to understanding economics, which most of mainstream theory ignores, is entrepreneurial creativity. Creativity entails innovation and this cannot be explained using standard models based upon the structure of physics because innovation is always surprising. Gilder makes the important point, "If creativity wasn't surprising, we could predict it and plan it—and we wouldn't need it. And socialism would work."

Information theory defines true information as surprise, and this means entrepreneurs must experiment and be able to fail, since failure also conveys information. Government intervention in the monetary system leads to government control over who gets credit, and removes the entrepreneurial surprise that is the basis for economic growth. Gilder's argument is that "capitalism is not chiefly an incentive system: It is an information and knowledge system." The effect of taxation is to deprive the entrepreneur of the income needed to undertake the process of continual innovation.

Gilder discusses the fact that reductions in income tax rates, in particular the tax on capital gains, results in both increased economic activity and in increased tax revenue. He discusses the increased taxation that is a basic part of Obamacare and its harmful effect on innovation. After comparing the Carter administration with the Reagan administration, he uses the history of post-World War II America to attack the recommendations of those who argue the economy requires large doses of government spending. Gilder closes with the admonition that a regime change that moves us from the path of big government toward one based on entrepreneurial information and innovation is quite possible if we seize the opportunity.

Daniel Mitchell addresses the income tax within the context of economic growth and a free society in "The Case for the Flat Tax."

The key to prosperity for everyone in society, especially the poor, is economic growth. This, he points out, entails adding to the capital stock. The current tax system actually reduces economic growth by creating double and triple taxation on savings, reducing the incentive to save and invest.

Mitchell clarifies that it is not just tax policy that determines economic growth: The rule of law, property rights, sound monetary policy, and limited regulations are also major factors. But the flat tax is a step in the right direction for a number of reasons. A flat tax with a low marginal rate will encourage entrepreneurial activity and risk taking that leads to innovation. It is equitable because everyone is treated the same: There are no loopholes, and there is a common tax rate for all. There is no double taxation, and its simplicity makes it easy for people to comply. It also reduces the amount of information that the government collects about the individual.

After making his case for the flat tax, Mitchell uses his 25 years of experience in Washington to emphasize that movement to a flat tax will be politically difficult. Each loophole has a special interest behind it, and congressmen like to affect the behavior of others by using the tax code. The challenge is for those who seek economic liberty and wealth for the masses to explain that upward mobility occurs in a growing economy with capital formation—something the flat tax is designed to encourage.

Finally, Mitchell brings up the national sales tax as an alternative. The national sales tax, or FairTax, is economically equivalent to the flat tax. While there are more technical reasons for this, given how income is designated under the flat tax, both types of tax only tax consumption. But the national sales tax would require the repeal of the Sixteenth Amendment along with a firm statement in the Constitution that the income tax would not be allowed, which would assuage Mitchell's fears that a national sales tax would simply be placed on top of an income tax.

John Linder directs his attention to the relative merits of a national sales tax, as opposed to the income tax, in "The Case for the FairTax." Linder argues that a national sales tax is more efficient than the income tax. Compliance costs of the income tax are very high,

$350 to $400 billion per year. The tax drives economic activity outside of the mainstream economy and creates inefficient allocation of resources as individuals and firms act to limit or avoid tax liability.

Linder points out that while the flat tax may have advantages over the current system, the political process will eventually restore the deductions and credits that the political class use to direct our activities, with the net result that any income tax reform will soon be undone. The FairTax, with its provisions for getting rid of the Sixteenth Amendment, would eliminate the income tax altogether. This proposal would not tax capital formation and would be less intrusive into Americans' private affairs than the income tax.

The income tax is a powerful tool for an expansive government and for those who would like to plan our economy centrally. The lessons that Mises taught us about the dangers of central planning and the benefits to the masses from a free market society are enhanced by studying the income tax, as the authors of this volume ably demonstrate.

GARY WOLFRAM
William E. Simon Professor of
Economics and Public Policy
Hillsdale College

Kendrick A. Clements

Woodrow Wilson, Progressivism, and the Sixteenth Amendment

Woodrow Wilson was a late convert to the idea of an income tax. In December 1906 President Theodore Roosevelt had urged the members of Congress to explore the "possibility of devising a constitutional income-tax law," and if that proved impossible, to pass a constitutional amendment to the Constitution.[1] Wilson, speaking in New York a few days later, rejected the idea. "In my opinion," he declared, "there is only one sort of taxation that is just, and that is taxation that does not discriminate." Government, he added, should not "punish a man for getting rich."[2]

When the United States was founded, no country had an income tax, not because there was any particular philosophical objection to it, but because no government had the capacity to gather and maintain detailed records on private incomes. A few years later, however, during the Wars of the French Revolution, the British inaugurated the first national income tax. During the War of 1812, the American Congress considered adopting an income tax, but the war ended before any law passed. The idea then lay dormant until 1861 when Congress passed the Revenue Act of 1861 in the hope of paying some of the costs of the Civil War. The act proved unworkable, and Congress returned to the issue the next year, passing the Tax Act of 1862, which required people who made up to $10,000 to pay three percent of their income, and those who made over $10,000 to pay five percent. The law, with various amendments, lasted until 1872, when Congress repealed it as part of general postwar tax cuts.[3]

No one raised any serious questions about the constitutionality of the Civil War income tax. So, in 1894, Democrats and Populists in Congress saw no problem in imposing a two-percent tax on incomes over $4,000 to replace revenues that would be lost when the Wilson–Gorman Act cut the tariff. Since the 1894 income tax affected only about five percent of Americans, however, conservatives denounced it as "class legislation." That in itself was not a sufficient justification for the Supreme Court to find the law unconstitutional, but in 1895 a court majority eager to strike it down reasoned that the tax was actually being levied on rents, and that it was thus a direct tax on land. Such taxes, under Article I, Section 2 of the Constitution, had to be apportioned among the states on the basis of population. The court conveniently ignored the fact that the incomes that would be taxed were mainly those of the new "robber barons" and came mostly from industry and finance, not from rents. Income tax advocates were disappointed with the decision, but the convoluted argument of *Pollock v. Farmers' Loan & Trust Company* led some of them to believe that it might be possible to draft a law that the court would find constitutional. Others concluded that a constitutional amendment would be necessary to legitimate the tax. Populists and other reformers, outraged by what they saw as an unhealthy concentration of wealth in the Northeast, urged Congress to re-pass the law and also proposed a constitutional amendment, but neither initiative went anywhere during the McKinley administration. Not until the early twentieth century and the rise of the Progressive movement led by Theodore Roosevelt at the national level did the issue revive.[4]

Heartened by the support of TR, reformers returned to the fight, and in 1909, when President Taft proposed a modest tariff reduction, Democrats and Progressive Republicans seized the opportunity to attach an income tax provision to the bill, again arguing that it would replace revenue lost through tariff cuts. Senator Nelson W.

Aldrich, arch-conservative chairman of the Senate Finance Committee, counted votes and concluded that the bill, with the income tax, would probably pass. In a hastily called conference with President Taft, the two agreed to propose a constitutional amendment legalizing the income tax. They felt sure that reformers would abandon the income tax provision of the tariff bill in return for the administration's support of the constitutional amendment, but that the amendment would never win the support of three-quarters of the states, the constitutional requirement for adoption. The proposed amendment did kill support for the income tax clause of the tariff bill, as Aldrich and Taft hoped, but the conservatives greatly underestimated popular support for the income tax idea. Over the next four years state after state approved the amendment, and on February 25, 1913, just nine days before Wilson's inauguration, Secretary of State Philander C. Knox declared it in effect.[5]

By the time Woodrow Wilson was elected governor of New Jersey as a reformer in 1910, he had begun to change his mind about the income tax. He now said privately that he supported the amendment but declined to endorse it publicly because some state legislators feared that a federal income tax would close off that source of revenue for the states. Pressed by William Jennings Bryan and others to speak out, he finally declared his support for the amendment in a message to the New Jersey legislature on March 20, 1911. On this, as on other issues, he was gradually moving to the left during these years.[6]

Yet if Wilson was slow to endorse the Sixteenth Amendment, he was quick to see its value to his program when he became president. One of his major campaign promises had been to slash the tariff and, just as in 1894, the income tax offered an obvious way to make up lost revenue. The income tax provision initially aroused little notice during the drafting of the tariff bill in early 1913. The main focus in both the White House and Congress was on tariff rates. Recognizing that setting duties on specific products was likely to be politically tricky, Wilson left the task of drafting the bill to Chairman Oscar W. Underwood and the other members of the House Ways and Means Committee. They wrestled with the issues, and on March 17 Underwood handed the president a draft bill. A week later Underwood and

Wilson spent four hours going over it. On the whole, the president was pleased, but he objected that the drafters had given in to the demands of their southern and western constituents in retaining high duties on farm products, sugar, wool, and leather boots and shoes. Such exceptions to across-the-board reductions, Wilson argued, would open the door to demands from all sorts of other interests for protection. If the subject of the income tax came up during this meeting, no record of it survives. Specific tariff schedules and fear that lobbyists would gut the bill occupied the forefront of the president's attention.[7]

At another meeting with Underwood on April 1 Wilson attempted to alleviate southern and western opposition to cuts by proposing that rates on food, leather, wool, and sugar be reduced gradually over a three-year span to cushion the blow on rural interests. Democrats on the Ways and Means Committee grumbled, but the president's strategy worked. When a special session of Congress convened on April 7 to consider the bill, it contained the terms Wilson wanted. On April 8 he broke precedent by appearing personally before a joint session of Congress to urge passage of the legislation.[8]

The theory behind tariff reduction was that it would reduce the cost of living by encouraging the importation of products that would be less costly than those produced by the so-called trusts, the giant corporations that dominated much of the American economy. Wilson anticipated that those corporations would lobby vigorously to retain their tariff advantages, but in the House party discipline prevailed, and the bill passed easily on May 8. In the Senate the situation was more difficult. Wilson kept up heavy pressure, going to the Capitol to meet with members of the Senate Finance Committee on April 9 and meeting with six western Democratic Senators on May 1. On May 26 he took his case to the public in a press conference. "This town is swarming with lobbyists, so you can't throw bricks in any direction without hitting one," he told reporters. He added that they were spending "money without limit" to defeat the tariff bill.[9]

Both Democrats and Republicans in the Senate expressed astonishment at Wilson's charges. They insisted they were unaware of any such concerted opposition to the bill. Republican Senator Albert Cummins of Iowa, hoping to embarrass the president by exposing the hollowness of his claims, proposed the creation of a special committee to investigate lobbying. But Wilson, refusing to back down, offered to provide the names of lobbyists, and Democrats rallied behind him, modifying Cummins' resolution to keep it safely in Democratic hands by entrusting the lobbying investigation to a subcommittee of the Senate Judiciary Committee chaired by Senator Lee S. Overman of North Carolina.[10]

The Overman Committee began work on June 2, but its investigation failed to expose any massive lobbying campaign by the trusts. It did reveal large holdings by many senators in sugar, cattle, and shoe and textile factories that suggested that they benefited from continued protectionism, and it brought to light a substantial lobbying operation by the beet sugar industry, but it did not find any significant lobbying by the great companies that most Americans thought of as "trusts." To the contrary, the giant Federal Sugar Refining Company actually endorsed even lower duties on cane sugar, and William E. Cody, former president of United States Steel, said, "I approve of the Underwood bill and do not believe that it will affect business unfavorably in this country except in isolated cases."[11]

The truth was that the Underwood Tariff came about twenty years too late to achieve the goals at which Wilson aimed. By 1913 the largest American companies had become so strong and efficient that they could compete anywhere in the world without special protection. Opposition to the Underwood bill came mainly from small and middle-sized companies fearful of adding foreign competition to that of the American giants. When Wilson fled to New Hampshire to escape Washington's August heat, he felt optimistic that overwhelming support by Senate Democrats would ensure the bill's speedy passage.

The lobbying controversy diverted attention from the income tax issue, which received little discussion either in Congress or in the press through most of the summer. Then, on August 26, Republican progressives thrust the matter into the forefront of Senate debate. Led by William E. Borah of Idaho, Joseph L. Bristow of Kansas, and Albert Cummins of Iowa, they proposed to reduce the tariff even more and to raise the income tax to replace the revenue. The next day Senator

Robert M. La Follette of Wisconsin introduced an amendment to the Underwood bill raising the maximum tax rate from 3 to 10 percent on incomes over $100,000. Although Senate Democrats united on August 28 to vote down the La Follette amendment, several of them soon began to have second thoughts. That evening, Henry F. Ashurst of Arizona, James A. Reed of Missouri, William H. Thompson of Kansas, and James K. Vardaman of Mississippi got together and demanded a meeting of the full Democratic caucus to reconsider the La Follette amendment. Panicked, Democratic leaders offered to raise the maximum rate to 7 percent and implored William Jennings Bryan to hold his supporters in line. After Bryan and Wilson issued a joint appeal, the caucus endorsed the compromise.[12]

One last challenge emerged when Republican progressives proposed to add a heavy inheritance tax to the measure, but that was defeated in a 58–12 vote, and on September 9 the Senate passed the bill. The president signed it into law on October 3.[13]

Although there is no doubt that by 1913 Wilson had come to believe that an income tax was a fair way to raise the money needed to support government activities, it is also clear that he viewed tariff reduction as his primary goal and had at most only vague ideas about the income tax that might serve to offset resulting revenue losses. Concerned about experts' warnings that tariff cuts might cost the government as much as $70 million a year, he approved the income tax as a way to fill the hole. In practice, the new tax fell far short of that goal. In 1914 it brought it only $28 million; in 1915, $41 million; and in 1916, $68 million. But as the war cut into American trade and customs receipts, and tax rates rose, administration and congressional leaders increasingly saw the income tax both as a way to replace what had been lost and as a major revenue source in itself. Without it, Wilson told Oscar Underwood in October 1914, the administration would have had to ask Congress for a special "war tax" to replace lost tariff revenue.[14]

By the autumn of 1915 Wilson had come to believe that the threat to American interests posed by the war in Europe (and especially on the Atlantic) required a program of military "preparedness." In his annual message to Congress on December 7, 1915, he argued that the U.S. "should be following an almost universal example of modern governments" in drawing "the greater part or even the whole of the revenues we need from the income taxes."[15] As in 1812 and 1861, war was creating an inexorable pressure to tap both individual and corporate incomes to pay for national defense.

The events that lay behind Wilson's decision to support the military buildup known as "preparedness" are familiar. The chain began with Germany's announcement in early 1915 that it would use submarines to enforce an unconventional blockade of the British Isles. Whereas a blockade normally required the stationing of warships near enemy harbors to stop, search, and, if appropriate, seize ships bearing certain proscribed cargoes that were headed for those ports, a submarine blockade was dramatically different. The fragile German submarines of 1915 were too vulnerable, and too few in number, to follow traditional rules of blockade. Instead, they roamed the sea lanes, attacking while submerged any ship they suspected of carrying goods to the enemy. Their captains, given the primitive technology available to them, could not always tell which ships belonged to belligerents and which to neutrals, and of course they had no way of knowing what any ship was carrying. The result of this situation was a series of incidents during the spring of 1915, culminating in the sinking of the *Lusitania* on May 7, with the deaths of 1,201 passengers and crew, including 128 Americans.

The submarine blockade presented Wilson with a stark choice. Either the United States must give up trade with the nations at war and keep its ships out of the war zone, or it must prepare to defend its trade rights. Slowly and reluctantly the president inched toward the latter choice during the summer and autumn of 1915.

Wilson estimated the cost of his proposed armaments program at $93,800,000 for fiscal year 1917. Along with other governmental obligations (including approximately $25,000,000 for work on the unfinished Panama Canal), he anticipated a total outlay for 1917 in the neighborhood of $300,000,000, which, if tax rates remained unchanged, meant a shortfall of about $112,000,000. Approximately half of the deficiency, he proposed, could be made up with taxes on gasoline, automobile horsepower, bank checks, pig iron, and fabricated iron and steel. The remainder, he argued, should come from the income tax.[16]

Progressives in Congress, fearful of war profiteering, reshaped Wilson's tax proposal. The Revenue Act of 1916 raised the maximum marginal income tax rate to 15 percent, but it also boosted the top income on which the rate applied from $500,000 to $2,000,000. More importantly, it raised the tax on net corporate incomes from 1 to 2 percent, inaugurated a federal inheritance tax ranging from 1 percent on the first $50,000 of estates and increasing to 10 percent on values over $5,000,000, and imposed a temporary -1/2 percent tax on munitions manufacturers. Although the bill did raise income taxes somewhat, it relied mainly on the inheritance, corporate, and munitions taxes.[17]

Wilson and the Democratic Platform of 1916 bragged that "[f]ederal taxation, which, under Republican legislation, was altogether a burden on consumption, upon the expenses of the poor as well as the rich, has been put in a way to be equalized by the adoption of an equitable income tax, which affords the government an elastic means of adjusting taxation to the fair tax-paying capacity of the individual citizen." Wilson biographer Arthur Link echoes the Democrats' boast, describing the 1916 law as the first truly progressive tax law in American history, a claim that seems somewhat overblown. The Republicans' 1916 presidential nominee, Charles Evans Hughes, although a moderate conservative, also endorsed the income tax.[18]

Thus it is clear that by 1916 dominant elements in both major parties had come to support the progressive income tax, not only for its capacity to raise large amounts of money at a critical moment in the nation's history, but for its social purposes as well. Supporters of the tax favored it in part because they believed that it helped to offset other, regressive taxes such as customs duties, which both taxed consumption and enriched American manufacturers who could charge higher prices for their products. Income tax supporters like Wilson pointed out that customs duties and excise or sales taxes (under which everyone paid the same tax rate on necessities) took a larger share of the income of the poor than of the wealthy. Advocates of progressive taxation also contended that the wealthy should pay more than the poor because they benefited more from services provided by government, such as the maintenance of order, than those who had less property to protect.[19] Whether Wilson accepted all of these arguments is unclear, but by 1916 he had certainly come to see the income tax as not only a fair means of supporting government, but as the fairest method.

Philosophical considerations aside, however, the main reason for the growing emphasis on the income tax was the astounding cost of the war. It would eventually cost the United States something like $50 billion, and federal spending leaped from $742 million in 1916 to $14 billion in 1918. Nothing but the income tax could provide anything like the amounts of money needed to support and equip the military.[20]

Wilson moved slowly from his 1906 opposition to any income tax to his full support of it a decade later. During the period that his opinion was evolving, leadership on the issue came not from the White House but from Progressives in the House and Senate. Their numbers and power grew dramatically between 1908 and 1915, and the structural reforms they pushed through Congress in that period enabled them to embody their ideas in legislation. They, not the president, became the national leaders on tax policy.

Three decades earlier, in his first book, *Congressional Government*, Wilson had described a situation in which Congress dominated the federal government and standing committees dominated Congress. In the early twentieth century the balance of power changed as the presidency grew more influential, the influence of the standing committees declined, and in the House of Representatives the speaker became so dominant that Speaker Joseph Cannon was referred to as a "czar." In 1910, however, the Democrats won control of both houses of Congress, and in the House of Representatives Republican Progressives joined the Democratic majority to curtail the speaker's power. Under the new power structure, the majority (Democratic) caucus rather than the speaker came to control the drafting and passage of legislation. The chairman of the House Ways and Means Committee both chaired the majority caucus and nominated the members of House committees, making him the dominant figure in the lower house.

Oscar W. Underwood of Alabama, the first majority leader under the new system, could influence all legislation in the House, but as chairman of the Ways and Means Committee he particularly controlled tax policy. After Underwood moved up to the Senate in 1915, his successor, Claude Kitchin of North Carolina, became the single most powerful House member. Only after 1919, when the Republicans took over and Joseph Fordney of Michigan became chairman of the committee, did the majority leader's power diminish significantly.[21]

Underwood delegated most of the task of writing the income tax provisions of the 1913 tariff bill to Representative Cordell Hull of Tennessee. As a young man, Hull had been a protégé of Benton McMillan, who drafted the 1894 income tax proposal, and he was a longtime student of foreign tax systems. A Bryan Democrat, Hull shared the Commoner's suspicion of big cities and big business. That an income tax would, on the whole, bear more heavily on urban than on rural incomes made the measure more appealing in his eyes. In addition to handling the complex task of drafting the income tax provisions of the tariff bill, Hull shepherded the completed legislation through the House. His task was made easier because most members of the House paid little attention to the income tax section of the tariff law, which occupied only eight pages in a more than 800-page bill and drew only two days of debate during the months the legislation was under consideration in the House.[22]

Claude Kitchin, who succeeded Underwood in 1915, was, like William Jennings Bryan, whom he had backed through three presidential campaigns, a strong supporter of the income tax, and he also shared Bryan's pacifist inclinations. Although Kitchin opposed preparedness and would vote against American entrance into the war in 1917, he immediately grasped that the international crisis provided a strong justification for raising tax rates on the wealthy. Charming, stubborn, and a master of House rules and practices, Kitchin seized the opportunity to make a graduated income tax the foundation of the tax bill of 1915, and repeated the process in the 1916 bill. When his Republican successor, Joseph Fordney, took over the Ways and Means Committee, he found there was little he could do to reverse the pattern Underwood, Hull, and Kitchin had established. "We need the money," Fordney admitted during the debate on the 1917 tax bill.[23]

Beyond the House, leaders in the Senate and in the Treasury Department also influenced tax policy during the Wilson years. Neither the Senate Finance Committee nor its chairman had nearly as much power as their House counterparts, but because of the Senate's tradition of unlimited debate, individual Senators could use the chamber's floor to press their ideas. In this case, a vigorous and articulate group of Democrats and Republican Progressives joined forces to urge the adoption of higher income and inheritance tax rates, as well as excess-profits taxes. As in the House, the group had a distinctly southern and midwestern rural outlook and tended to regard urban and eastern moneyed interests with deep suspicion. Within the president's cabinet, Treasury Secretary William Gibbs McAdoo, a Tennessean who was also Wilson's son-in-law, insisted that "if we are to preserve the soundness and stability of our financial structure, we must raise not less than one-third of our expenditures by taxation," and he emphasized that he favored taxes that raised as much money as possible, regardless of whether they "hurt our pockets or involve sacrifices."[24] Other members of the cabinet frequently expressed similar views. Patriotism, they argued, demanded shared sacrifice, but many of them also found in the cause of the income tax an opportunity to refight old sectional and economic battles.

In 1917, as the United States moved toward war, Congress first hoped to cover increasing military expenses by boosting inheritance and excess profits taxes, but by the time the president asked for a declaration of war in April it was obvious that only the income tax could generate anywhere near enough revenue. Moreover, the beginning of war drove up government expenditures at the same time that an economic boom began to boost profits and incomes for some individuals and companies enormously, while leaving others behind.[25] The progressive rates of the income tax became an advantage in this situation, forcing those who benefited most to pay more while easing the burden on those who lagged behind. That principle was embodied in the War Revenue Act of 1917, which pushed the top rate to 67 percent on incomes over $2,000,000 (but exempted the first $4,000 of couples' and the first $3,000 of singles' income). In addition, Congress created a special fund for military and naval purposes, authorizing an excess-profits tax on businesses and an increase in the inheritance tax to pay for it. The next year the top tax rate went up again, to 77 percent on incomes over $1,000,000. The rate dropped to 73 percent in 1919 and remained at that level through 1921, despite the end of hostilities in November 1918.[26]

Debate about the War Revenue Act of 1917 in particular took place within the context of debate about the first American draft law. If young men were expected to give up their civilian status and perhaps even lose their lives for $30 a month, there was a broad bipartisan consensus that there should also be a "conscription of wealth" so that those who were profiting economically from the conflict would have to bear a fair share of its burden.[27]

As the drafters of the tax laws intended, the effect of these tax increases on federal income was dramatic. Federal revenues rose above $1 billion for the first time in 1917 and climbed to over $6.5 billion in 1920 before postwar tax reductions took effect.[28] Yet despite the striking increases in revenue resulting from the income tax, the administration's hope of paying at least half of the costs of the war from current taxation, although endorsed by leading economists, proved out of reach. Treasury Secretary McAdoo warned solemnly that borrowing heavily would drive up interest rates and inflation, bringing "ultimate destruction upon the country," but Congress was unwilling to raise rates to the near-confiscatory levels that McAdoo's argument implied. And in the end, even McAdoo's pessimistic predictions about what the war would cost proved too low. He revised his estimates upward several times, ultimately more than tripling his original figure, but still the conflict's prodigious appetite for money led to growing deficits in 1917 ($853.4 million), 1918 ($9 billion), and 1919 ($13.4 billion).[29] Paying down the national debt that resulted from the war became a strong argument for keeping tax rates substantially higher throughout the 1920s than in prewar years.

Throughout American history prior to 1920 war provided the most powerful justification for the income tax. Because war both increased government expenses and reduced revenues from the tariff, which before 1913 provided approximately one-half of government income, lawmakers turned to the income tax to replace and supplement traditional sources of federal revenue in nearly every war after the Revolution. The Constitution said nothing about the tax, and prior to 1895, when the Supreme Court declared it unconstitutional, legislators accepted it readily when the government needed to increase its income.

As it happened, the Supreme Court's 1895 ruling coincided with a new political argument for a federal income tax—the sharp rural-urban conflict known as Populism. In the eyes of Populists and their allies, the federal government had been captured by eastern commercial and industrial interests, who were using their power to further enrich themselves by using the tariff to block the admission of low-cost foreign goods that would compete with the products of the "trusts." Reformers saw the income tax less as a way of increasing government revenue than as a device to redress the balance between farmers and eastern urbanites. Thus the Populist Party platform of 1892 strongly endorsed the idea of a graduated income tax, and William Jennings Bryan made the concept a central part of the Democratic Party's program when he ran for president in 1896. In the rural areas of the South and the Midwest, the income tax soon caught on as a goal for reformers from both major parties as well as the Populists. More than a philosophical debate, the issue became a part of sectional conflict.

Although Woodrow Wilson shared the South's traditional antipathy to the protective tariff, he did not embrace the Populists nor their enthusiasm for the income tax. In a widely quoted letter, he declared in 1908 that he would like to see William Jennings Bryan knocked into a "cocked hat," and when Theodore Roosevelt embraced the income tax in 1906, Wilson denounced the idea. Even after the rapid progress toward the ratification of the Sixteenth Amendment showed widespread support for the tax among Americans, Wilson was slow to jump on the bandwagon. Not until 1911, as he pondered a run for the presidency, did he urge the New Jersey legislature to approve the constitutional amendment. In 1913, it is true, he endorsed the income tax clause in the Underwood tariff bill, but at the lowest possible level, and only as a way to make up lost revenue from tariff reduction. When Democratic and Republican Progressives from the South and Midwest tried to increase tax rates sharply as the Senate debated the tariff bill, Wilson fought successfully to block their efforts. In the end, the 1913 tax rate was set so low that it did not bring in enough money to replace lost tariff income.

Wilson really embraced the income tax only in 1915, when he decided that the U.S. must be able to defend its foreign trade and investments, which were threatened by the escalating violence of World War I. That defense required a military buildup, especially of the Navy, he argued, and he predicted that it would cost nearly $100 million in the first year alone. That was a staggering sum at a time when the entire U.S. budget was less than $300 million. Paying for "preparedness," he concluded, required that the United States follow the lead of other nations and adopt a sharply graduated income tax. That policy, he argued when he ran for reelection in 1916, was not only necessitated by sharply rising defense costs, but it was fair because it apportioned the costs of government among those who could best afford to pay those costs. Moreover, since the war's disruption of the economy had created a situation where some Americans were making unprecedented profits while workers faced a rising cost of living, the income tax offered a way to balance the burden.

War thus released the income tax genie from its bottle, and its power was so enormous that putting it back proved impossible. When the Republicans took over Congress and the White House in the 1920s, they promised to cut taxes and shrink the size and activities of government, but even the most conservative members of the administration, such as Treasury Secretary Andrew Mellon, favored retaining an income tax to pay off war debt and to provide money to protect growing American economic interests overseas. Other members of the administration saw the tax as desirable to fund activities that even liberals had not suggested before the war. Agriculture Secretary Henry C. Wallace, for example, wanted the federal government to subsidize struggling farmers, while Commerce Secretary Herbert Hoover proposed massive new infrastructure expenditures that he contended would benefit industry and trade as well as agriculture. Despite five federal tax cuts during the 1920s, government revenues—and expenditures—remained at least four times as great during that decade as in prewar years, and although the top marginal rate dropped from over 70 percent to 25 percent, the Republicans never proposed eliminating the tax entirely or even cutting it back to the prewar level of 7 percent.

Woodrow Wilson, it is true, had presided over the first major application of the income tax idea in American history, but it was under the conservative Republican administrations of the 1920s that it became a normal and permanent part of government policy in peacetime. As Cordell Hull wrote many years later, the wartime income tax passed by the Wilson administration "permanently established" the principle of the tax and "laid the cornerstone for the structure of government financing [for] the First World War, the peace period following, and the Second World War." Even more than war financing, it was the peaceful period between the wars that normalized the income tax as a permanent part of American life.[30]

Notes

1. Arthur S. Link et al., eds., *The Papers of Woodrow Wilson*, vol. 16, *1905–1907* (Princeton, NJ: Princeton University Press, 1973), 531n3.
2. Woodrow Wilson, address to the Southern Society of New York, as reported in *The New York Times*, December 15, 1906, ibid., 530.
3. http://history1900sabout.com/od/1910s/a/incometax.htm. Burton Fulsom argues that the Founders deliberately worded the Constitution in such a way as to rule out an income tax. Certainly it is true that, as he notes, Madison and other Founders were concerned both about the dangers of faction and the possibility that the majority would oppress the minority, but I doubt they had the income tax in mind, since no such tax had yet been invented. See Burton W. Fulsom, Jr., "The Progressive Income Tax in U.S. History: The Root of Much Evil," *Freeman* 53 (May 2003).
4. Jerold L. Waltman, *Political Origins of the U.S. Income Tax* (Jackson: University Press of Mississippi, 1985), 3–5.
5. Ibid., 5–6; http://www.ourdocuments.gov/doc.php?flash=true&doc=57.
6. Link et al., *The Papers of Woodrow Wilson*, vol. 22, *1910–1911* (Princeton, NJ: Princeton University Press, 1976), 434, 465, 511–12. As it turned out, the legislature voted down the income tax amendment on the same day that it

received Wilson's measure endorsing it (March 20, 1911) and did not approve the amendment until February 4, 1913. Wilson urged the amendment on the legislature for a second time in a message to the state senate on April 4, 1911, ibid., 534–35, and again on February 26, 1912, ibid., vol. 24, *1912* (Princeton, NJ: Princeton University Press, 1977), 216–17, and his final message to the legislature as he prepared to move to Washington, January 14, 1913, ibid., vol. 27, *1913* (Princeton, NJ: Princeton University Press, 1978), 54.

7. Kendrick A. Clements, *Woodrow Wilson, World Statesman* (Boston: Twayne Publishers, 1987), 104–5.

8. Ibid., 105.

9. Link et al., *The Papers of Woodrow Wilson*, vol. 27 (1978), 472, 473.

10. Clements, *Wilson*, 106.

11. Frank Burdick, "Woodrow Wilson and the Underwood Tariff," *Mid-America* 50 (October 1968): 280.

12. Link et al., *The Papers of Woodrow Wilson*, vol. 28, *1913* (Princeton, NJ: Princeton University Press, 1978), 247–48, 254, 258; Clements, *Wilson*, 107–8. As finally adopted, the maximum rate was 6 percent on incomes over $500,000. See http://fraser.stlouisfed.org/docs/publications/income/pages/33309_1925-1929.pdf

13. Clements, *Wilson*, 108–9.

14. *Historical Statistics of the United States, Millennial Edition* (2006), Table Ea588; Davis Rich Dewey, *Financial History of the United States*, 12th ed. (NY: Longmans, Green & Co., 1936), 490–91; Wilson to Underwood, October 17, 1914, Link et al., *The Papers of Woodrow Wilson*, vol. 31, *September 6–December 31, 1914* (Princeton, NJ: Princeton University Press, 1979), 170; Don Wolfensberger, "Woodrow Wilson, Congress, and the Income Tax," An Introductory Essay for the Congress Project Seminar on "Congress and Tax Policy," Woodrow Wilson International Center for Scholars, Tuesday, March 16, 2004, at www.Wilsoncenter.org/sites/default/files/ACF18.pdf.

15. Link et al., *The Papers of Woodrow Wilson*, vol. 35, *October 1, 1915–January 27, 1916* (Princeton, NJ: Princeton University Press, 1980), 305. Wilson was overly optimistic. In the end, taxes paid only about one-third of the total cost (including loans to foreign governments) of the war, or about 43 percent of the cost exclusive of foreign loans. See Dewey, *Financial History*, 511.

16. Link et al., *The Papers of Woodrow Wilson*, vol. 35 (1980), 303–6.

17. Link et al., *The Papers of Woodrow Wilson*, vol. 38, *August 7–November 19, 1916* (Princeton, NJ: Princeton University Press, 1982), 51–52n1, 130; ibid., vol. 37, *May 9–August 7, 1916* (Princeton, NJ: Princeton University Press, 1981), 192; Wolfensberger, "Woodrow Wilson, Congress, and the Income Tax," 9–10.

18. http://fraser.stlouisfed.org/docs/publications/income/pages/33309_1925-1929.pdf. Governor Hughes had submitted the Sixteenth Amendment to the New York legislature in January 1910 with the recommendation that it be rejected, not because he opposed the income tax, but because he feared that its wording

would make it possible for Congress to tax revenue from state and municipal bonds that were essential to funding public improvements. See ibid., 203n5.

19. Waltman, *Political Origins of the U.S. Income Tax*, 10–11. Waltman is here describing arguments for the income tax in general, but it is clear that Wilson accepted some if not all of them.

20. Wolfensberger, "Woodrow Wilson, Congress, and the Income Tax," 10.

21. Waltman, *Political Origins of the U.S. Income Tax*, 18–19; Wolfensberger, "Woodrow Wilson, Congress, and the Income Tax," 4.

22. Waltman, ibid., 34–35; Wolfensberger, ibid., 5–6.

23. Waltman, ibid.; Wolfensberger, ibid., 11.

24. Waltman, ibid., 21; Lansing to Wilson, May 23, 1916, Link et al., *The Papers of Woodrow Wilson*, vol. 48, *May 13–July 17, 1918* (Princeton, NJ: Princeton University Press, 1983), 122. I have reversed the order of the phrases.

25. Waltman, *Political Origins of the U.S. Income Tax*, 42.

26. http://fraser.stlouisfed.org/docs/publications/income/pages/33309_1925-1929.pdf. Secretary of Agriculture David F. Houston and Treasury Secretary William Gibbs McAdoo believed that the $4,000 exemption for couples and the $3,000 exemption for singles were too high, but Congress, unwilling to antagonize the middle class, refused to lower the exemptions. See Link et al., *The Papers of Woodrow Wilson*, vol. 37 (1981), 376–77.

27. Waltman, *Political Origins of the U.S. Income Tax*, 43.

28. *Historical Statistics of the United States, Millennial Edition* (2006), Table Ea588.

29. Ibid., Table Ea584. For the views of economists Oliver M. W. Sprague and John R. Commons, see Link et al., *The Papers of Woodrow Wilson*, vol. 41, *January 24–April 6, 1917* (Princeton, NJ: Princeton University Press, 1983), 448; McAdoo to Wilson, May 23, 1918, ibid., 48:122. It is worth noting that although the Republican administration of the 1920s cut taxes (and hence reduced government revenues), government spending continued to average two to three times greater than in prewar years.

30. Hull quoted in Wolfensberger, "Woodrow Wilson, Congress, and the Income Tax," 11.

Amity Shlaes

Calvin Coolidge and the Moral Case for Economy

With the federal debt spiraling out of control, many Americans sense an urgent need to find a political leader who is able to say "no" to spending. Yet they fear that finding such a leader is impossible. Conservatives long for another Ronald Reagan. But is Reagan the right model? He was of course a tax cutter, reducing the top marginal rate from 70 to 28 percent. But his tax cuts—which vindicated supply-side economics by vastly increasing federal revenue—were bought partly through a bargain with Democrats who were eager to spend that revenue. Reagan was no budget cutter—indeed, the federal budget rose by over a third during his administration.[1]

An alternative model for conservatives is Calvin Coolidge. President from 1923 to 1929, Coolidge sustained a budget surplus and left office with a smaller budget than the one he inherited. Over the same period, America experienced a proliferation of jobs, a dramatic increase in the standard of living, higher wages, and three to four percent annual economic growth. And the key to this was Coolidge's penchant for saying "no." If Reagan was the Great Communicator, Coolidge was the Great Refrainer.

19

Enter Coolidge

Following World War I, the federal debt stood ten times higher than before the war, and it was widely understood that the debt burden would become unbearable if interest rates rose. At the same time, the top income tax rate was over 70 percent, veterans were having trouble finding work, prices had risen while wages lagged, and workers in Seattle, New York, and Boston were talking revolution and taking to the streets.

The Woodrow Wilson administration had nationalized the railroads for a time at the end of the war, and had encouraged stock exchanges to shut down for a time, and Progressives were now pushing for state or even federal control of water power and electricity. The business outlook was grim, and one of the biggest underlying problems was the lack of an orderly budgeting process: Congress brought proposals to the White House willy-nilly, and they were customarily approved. The Republican Party's response in the 1920 election was to campaign for smaller government and for a return to what its presidential candidate, Warren Harding, dubbed "normalcy"—a curtailing of government interference in the economy to create a predictable environment in which business could confidently operate.

Calvin Coolidge, a Massachusetts governor who had gained a national reputation by facing down a Boston police strike—"There is no right to strike against the public safety by anybody, anywhere, any time,"[2] he had declared—was chosen to be Harding's running mate. And following their victory, Harding's inaugural address set a different tone from that of the outgoing Wilson administration (and from that of the Obama administration today): "No altered system," Harding said, "will work a miracle. Any wild experiment will only add to the confusion. Our best assurance lies in efficient administration of our proven system."

One of Harding's first steps was to shepherd through Congress the Budget and Accounting Act of 1921, under which the executive branch gained authority over and took responsibility for the budget, even to the point of being able to impound money after it was budgeted. This legislation also gave the executive branch a special budget bureau—the forerunner to today's Office of Management and Budget—over which Harding named a flamboyant Brigadier General, Charles Dawes, as director. Together they proceeded to summon department staff and their bosses to semiannual meetings at Continental Hall, where Dawes cajoled and shamed them into making spending cuts. In addition, Harding pushed through a tax cut, lowering the top rate to 58 percent; and in a move toward privatization, he proposed to sell off naval petroleum reserves in Wyoming to private companies.

Unfortunately, some of the men Harding appointed to key jobs proved susceptible to favoritism or bribery, and his administration soon became embroiled in scandal. In one instance, the cause of privatization sustained damage when it became clear that secret deals had taken place in the leasing of oil reserves at Teapot Dome. Then in the summer of 1923, during a trip out West to get away from the scandals and prepare for a new presidential campaign, Harding died suddenly.

Enter Coolidge, whose personality was at first deemed a negative—his face, Alice Roosevelt Longworth said, "looked as though he had been weaned on a pickle." But canny political leaders, including Supreme Court Justice and former President William Howard Taft, quickly came to respect the new president. Secretary of State Charles Evans Hughes, after visiting the White House a few times that August, noted that whereas Harding had never been alone, Coolidge often was; that whereas Harding was partial to group decisions, Coolidge made decisions himself; and most important, that whereas Harding's customary answer was "yes," Coolidge's was "no."[3]

The former governor of Massachusetts was in his element when it came to budgeting. Within 24 hours of arriving back in Washington after Harding's death, he met with his own budget director, Herbert Lord, and together they went on offense, announcing deepened cuts in two politically sensitive areas: spending on veterans and District of Columbia public works. In his public statements, Coolidge made clear he would have scant patience with anyone who didn't go along: "We must have no carelessness in our dealings with public property or the expenditure of public money. Such a condition is characteristic of undeveloped people, or of a decadent generation."[4]

If Harding's budget meetings had been rough, Coolidge's were rougher. Lord first advertised a "Two Percent Club," for executive branch staffers who managed to save two percent in their budgets. Then a "One Percent Club," for those who had achieved two or more already. And finally a "Woodpecker Club," for department heads who kept chipping away. Coolidge did not even find it beneath his pay grade to look at the use of pencils in the government: "I don't know if I ever indicated to the conference that the cost of lead pencils to the government per year is about $125,000," he instructed the press in 1926.[5] "I am for economy, and after that I am for more economy," he told voters.[6]

Coolidge in Command

"It is much more important to kill bad bills than to pass good ones," Coolidge had once advised his father. And indeed, while Harding had vetoed only six bills, Coolidge vetoed 50—including farming subsidies, even though he came from farming country. ("Farmers never had made much money," he told a guest, and he didn't see there was much the government could rightly do about it.)[7] He also vetoed veterans' pensions and government entry into the utilities sector.

Perhaps reflecting his temperament, Coolidge favored the pocket veto—a way for the president to reject a bill without a veto message and without affording Congress a chance to override a veto. Grover Cleveland, who Coolidge admired, had used this veto in his day, as had Theodore Roosevelt. But Coolidge raised its use to an art form. The *New York Times* referred to it as "disapproval by inaction."[8]

Gaining public acceptance of having a Scrooge as president required playing the role of Scrooge consistently. Coolidge took care to do so, visiting his saving habit on everyone around him. It was at the White House dinner table, for instance, that Coolidge's attack on "pork" became literal: At one point the housekeeper proudly showed the President the spread for a big dinner, and instead of receiving praise she was scolded for serving "an awful lot of ham."[9] She departed soon after.

The Hurricane Katrina of the Coolidge years, the great Mississippi River flood of 1927, wiped out many areas of the South. Yet

Coolidge pointedly chose not to visit the devastated areas—sending Commerce Secretary Herbert Hoover in his place—out of concern that a presidential visit might encourage the idea of federal spending on disaster relief, for which there were already advocates in Congress. This triggered resentment, which Senator Thaddeus Caraway of Arkansas expressed in personal terms: "I venture to say that if a similar disaster had affected New England the President would have had no hesitation in calling an extra session. Unfortunately he was unable to visualize the situation."[10] But soon thereafter floods tore across Vermont, the state where Coolidge had spent his childhood, and calls for him to visit grew loud—to no avail. "He can't do for his own, you see, more than he did for the others," as one Vermonter explained.[11] Vermont, like Arkansas, would have to recover without federal intervention.

In doing research for my new biography of Coolidge, I reviewed his presidential appointment books and found a clue as to why he was able to be so consistent: sheer discipline. Coolidge and his budget director met every Friday morning before cabinet meetings to identify budget cuts and discuss how to say "no" to the requests of cabinet members. Most presidents give in after a time—Eisenhower being a good example—but Coolidge did not, despite the budget surpluses during his presidency. He held 14 meetings with his budget director after coming to office in late 1923, 55 meetings in 1924, 52 in 1925, 63 in 1926, and 51 in 1927.

In a conference call with Jewish philanthropists, Coolidge explained his consistency this way: "I believe in budgets. I want other people to believe in them. I have had a small one to run my own home; and besides that, I am the head of the organization that makes the greatest of all budgets, that of the United States government. Do you wonder then that at times I dream of balance sheets and sinking funds, and deficits and tax rates and all the rest?"[12]

The Purpose of Tax Cuts

Speaking of tax rates, in December 1923, Coolidge and Treasury Secretary Andrew Mellon launched a campaign to lower top rates from the fifties to the twenties. Mellon believed, and informed Coolidge, that these cuts might result in additional revenue. This was referred to as "scientific taxation"—an early formulation of the Laffer Curve. And Coolidge passed the word on: "Experience does not show that the higher rate produces the larger revenue. Experience is all the other way," he said in a speech in early 1924. "When the surtax on incomes of $300,000 and over was but 10 percent, the revenue was about the same as it was at 65 percent."[13]

Mellon and Coolidge did not win all they sought. The top rate of the final law was in the forties. But even this reduction yielded results—more money flowing into the Treasury—suggesting that "scientific taxation" worked. By 1926, Coolidge was able to sign legislation that brought the top marginal rate down to 25 percent, and to do so retroactively.

Today's Republicans tend to take pleasure when the Laffer Curve is vindicated and more money flows into government as a result of tax cuts. Indeed, this idea of "scientific taxation" is often used to attempt to get Democrats to go along with tax cuts, as if those cuts are an end in themselves. By contrast, the specter of increased federal revenue rendered Coolidge anxious, personally and politically—so much so that he considered *foregoing* the rate cuts: "While I am exceedingly interested in having tax reduction . . . it can only be brought about as a result of economy," he said at one point.[14] He would not put tax cuts before budget reduction, insisting on twinning the two goals. To underscore the point, twin lion cubs given to Coolidge by the mayor of Johannesburg were named "Budget Bureau" and "Tax Reduction."

In short, Coolidge didn't favor tax cuts as a means to increase revenue or to buy off Democrats. He favored them because they took government, the people's servant, out of the way of the people. And this sense of government as servant extended to his own office. Senator Selden Spencer once took a walk with Coolidge around the White House grounds. To cheer the President up, Spencer pointed to the White House and asked playfully, "Who lives there?" "Nobody," Coolidge replied. "They just come and go."[15]

This view of government and his attendant insistence on economy made Coolidge few friends in Washington—a fact illustrated by notes kept by White House usher Ike Hoover. These notes record the excuses given by lawmakers for not attending breakfasts hosted by Coolidge at the White House: "Senator Heflin: Regrets, sick. Senator Norris: Unable to Locate. Senator Pittman: Regrets, sick. Senator Reed, of Missouri: Regrets, sick friend." But as unpopular as he was in Washington, Coolidge proved enormously popular with voters. In 1924, the Progressive Party ran on a platform of government ownership of public power and a return to government ownership of railroads. Many thought the Progressive Party might split the Republican vote as it had in 1912, handing the presidency to the Democrats. As it happened, Progressive candidate Robert La Follette indeed claimed more than 16 percent of the vote. Yet Coolidge won with an absolute majority, gaining more votes than the Progressive and the Democrat combined. And in 1928, when Coolidge decided not to run for reelection despite the urging of party leaders who looked on his reelection as a sure bet, Herbert Hoover successfully ran on a pledge to continue Coolidge's policies.

Unfortunately, Hoover didn't live up to his pledge. Critics often confuse Hoover's policies with Coolidge's and complain that the latter did not prevent the Great Depression. That is an argument I take up at length in my previous book, *The Forgotten Man*, and is a topic for another day. Here let me just say that the Great Depression was as great and as long in duration as it was because, as economist Benjamin Anderson put it, the government under both Hoover and Franklin Roosevelt, unlike under Coolidge, chose to "play God."

Beyond the inspiration of Coolidge's example of principle and consistency, what are the lessons of his story that are relevant to our current situation? One certainly has to do with the mechanism of budgeting: The Budget and Accounting Act of 1921 provided a means for Harding and Coolidge to control the budget and the nation's debt, and at the same time gave the people the ability to hold someone responsible. That law was gutted in the 1970s, when it became collateral damage in the anti-executive fervor following Watergate. The law that replaced it tilted budget authority back to Congress and has led to over-spending and lack of responsibility.

A second lesson concerns how we look at tax rates. When tax rates are set and judged according to how much revenue they bring in due to the Laffer Curve—which is how most of today's tax cutters present them, thereby agreeing with tax hikers that the goal of tax policy is to increase revenue—tax policy can become a mechanism to expand government. The goals of legitimate government—American freedom and prosperity—are left by the wayside. Thus the best case for lower taxes is the moral case—and as Coolidge well understood, a moral tax policy demands tough budgeting.

Finally, a lesson about politics. The popularity of Harding and Coolidge, and the success of their policies—especially Coolidge's —following a long period of Progressive ascendancy, should give today's conservatives hope. Coolidge in the 1920s, like Grover Cleveland in the previous century, distinguished government austerity from private-sector austerity, combined a policy of deficit cuts with one of tax cuts, and made a moral case for saying "no." A political leader who does the same today is likely to find an electorate more inclined to respond "yes" than he or she expects.

Footnotes

1. Table 1.3 historical tables: http://www.whitehouse.gov/sites/default/files/omb/budget/fy2013/assets/hist.pdf.
2. Calvin Coolidge, *Have Faith in Massachusetts* (New York: Houghton Mifflin, 1919), 223.
3. Merlo J. Pusey, *Charles Evans Hughes* (New York: Macmillan, 1951).
4. Calvin Coolidge, "Economy in the Interest of All," Address at the Meeting of the Business Organization of the Government, June 30, 1924: http://www.presidency.ucsb.edu/calvin_coolidge.php.
5. Calvin Coolidge, Presidential Press Conference, November 19, 1926 in Howard H. Quint and Robert H. Ferrel, editors, *The Talkative President: The Off-The-Record Press Conferences of Calvin Coolidge* (Amherst: University of Massachusetts Press, 1964).
6. Calvin Coolidge, "Economy in the Interest of All."
7. Robert H. Ferrell, *The Presidency of Calvin Coolidge* (Lawrence: University of Kansas, 1998), 86.
8. Richard V. Oulahan, "Congress Ends Session With Senate in Uproar, " *New York Times* (May 30, 1928):1.
9. Elizabeth Jaffray, *Secrets of the White House* (New York: Cosmoplitan Book Press, 1927), 105.

10. Carlisle Bargeron, "Coolidge Refusal of Extra Session Roils Democrats," *Washington Post* (September 16, 1927).
11. "Vermont Folk," *Boston Globe* (November 13, 1927).
12. Calvin Coolidge, Telephone Remarks to the Federation of Jewish Philanthropic Societies of New York City, Assembled at the Hotel Pennsylvania, October 26, 1924: http://www.presidency.ucsb.edu/calvin_coolidge.php.
13. "Will Permit No Politics," *New York Times* (February 13, 1924).
14. *The Talkative President*, 109.
15. Senator Selden Spencer in Edward Connery Lathem, ed., *Meet Calvin Coolidge: The Man Behind the Myth* (Brattleboro, VT: Stephen Greene Press, 1960), 148.

W. ELLIOT BROWNLEE

The Federal Income Tax: The First Hundred Years

As an historian who has been studying the modern federal income tax for many years, the centennial anniversary of the tax is an occasion not of celebration, but rather of opportunity to use history to understand the fiscal dilemmas that currently confront the United States. To resolve our problems the nation will have to consider comprehensive tax reform, among other measures. To do that intelligently, tax reformers and the public at large ought to know what history has to tell us about how Americans have reformed, or failed to reform, the income tax over the last century.

The federal income tax actually arrived on the scene much earlier than 1913. Its first appearance was in 1861, during the early months of the Civil War, and it survived until 1872. In 1894, the federal government reinstated an income tax. We would have celebrated the first century of the income tax in 1994 had the Supreme Court not struck it down in *Pollock v. Farmers' Loan & Trust Company* in 1895. That did, however, set the stage for the passage of the Sixteenth Amendment nearly twenty years later. The century of federal income tax history I will discuss began in 1913 with the passage of the Underwood Tariff soon after President Woodrow Wilson took office.

Wilson was a Democrat who was elected in an unusual three-way race between the Republican candidate William Howard Taft and Theodore Roosevelt, the candidate of the short-lived Progressive Party. During that campaign of 1912, the income tax was never really an issue. All three candidates were silent on the topic, sharing the view that a broad popular consensus would ratify the Sixteenth Amendment. Subsequently, the enactment of the income tax in 1913 within the Underwood Tariff required little exercise of presidential influence by Wilson.

The provisions of the new tax only faintly suggested what the income tax would become over the next century. The new law imposed a so-called "normal" tax of one percent on the taxable net income of every U.S. citizen. It provided each taxpaying family with an exemption of $3,000, with an additional exemption of $1,000 for spouses. In addition, the legislation established a surtax, or additional tax, with progressive rates on net incomes above $20,000, rising from an additional one percent on incomes above $20,000 to six percent above $500,000. Collection of the tax followed the English model of stoppage, or collection at the source. Under this system, whoever paid wages, salaries, interest, dividends, and rents was obliged to deduct the taxes from the payments and turn them over to the U.S. Treasury. (Corporations would pay an income tax also—a one-percent flat rate on their net income.)

What these numbers meant was that initially only about one to two percent of American families paid income tax: in other words, only those who were among the most wealthy. The tax rates, however, were too low to generate much revenue. There is almost no evidence that in 1913 either Wilson or the congressional leadership viewed the tax as the core instrument for financing future naval expenditures, armies, future wars, or welfare-state initiatives. The tax seemed designed primarily to supplement weakening tariff revenues. But the incomes of those who would pay the income tax suggested that the Wilson administration and Congress had another objective in mind— that of shifting the tax burden to the wealthiest Americans. While the rates were too low to replace a significant portion of the revenues garnered through other taxes—regressive tariffs and regressive "sin taxes" on alcohol and tobacco—Wilson and Congress had inserted the thin edge of the wedge. Certainly by supporting the graduated feature of the 1913 income tax, Wilson moved beyond his heroes, the nineteenth-century British liberals such as William Gladstone, who favored income taxes but were often troubled by graduated rates. The ethical call behind the movement that had produced the 1913 income tax embraced the principle of taxation according to "ability to pay." To its champions, this meant progressive taxation that would offset the regressive effects of the tariffs and consumption taxes on which the federal government had relied since the Civil War.

The criterion of "ability to pay" appealed to many people in Wilson's day, as it does in our own. But it has always been far more of a cliché, or political slogan, than a clear guide for policymakers. Many economists have offered formulations of the criteria.[1] But in practice "ability to pay" has always been more a platitude than an operational standard. Wilson himself recognized this, advising Furnifold M. Simmons, chair of the Senate Finance Committee, to be cautious in setting the rates for the new income tax. "Individual judgments will naturally differ," Wilson told Simmons, "with regard to the burden it is fair to lay upon incomes which run above the usual levels."[2] Wilson knew that Americans had widely varying interpretations of what "ability to pay" means, and about how progressive the tax system or a particular tax should be.

Woodrow Wilson had to abandon his caution, however, when he faced the financial demands of intervention in World War I. The disruption of international trade after 1914 ruined the tariff as a revenue source, and the experience of relying on internal consumption taxes had proved an economic and administrative disaster during the Civil War. The Treasury lacked the means to reach out into the countryside and small towns of America and determine the incomes of most American families and small businesses, and then collect the taxes on those incomes. The only administratively feasible sources of massive income tax revenues at this time were the wealthier American families and corporations. Moreover, Americans of modest means, both in urban and rural communities, applauded "soaking the rich" as a means of wartime finance. Particularly compelling to progressive politicians, including Wilson, and their supporters was the opportunity to use an expanded corporate income tax as a means of controlling or even rolling-back what appeared to be monopoly profits. In addition, many progressive politicians blamed financial capitalism, and its ties with English financial power, for having involved the United States in the European war.

With the passage of the Revenue Act of 1916, the modest income tax of 1913 became an expansive effort to impose the progressive taxation of personal and corporate income, and of estates, to share in wartime sacrifices, to redistribute social power, and to expand economic opportunity. Subsequent wartime tax increases imposed marginal rates ranging between 15 to 77 percent on the wealthiest one percent of American families. In 1918, their effective rates averaged 15 percent, having increased from 3 percent in 1916.[3] This one percent of American families accounted for about 80 percent of the revenues from the personal income tax, and only the wealthiest 15 percent of families paid any income tax. Meanwhile, corporations faced a basic corporate tax rate of 12 percent and a graduated tax from 30 to 65 percent on so-called "excess profits"—business profits above a bureaucratically determined "normal" rate of return. The excess-profits tax accounted for about two-thirds of all federal tax revenues during World War I and added to the tax burden that the personal income tax placed on the rich. Among the belligerents, only the United States and Canada taxed excess profits this way, and only the United States placed excess profits taxes at the center of wartime finance.

The wartime experiments with progressive income taxation dramatically transformed the political economy of taxation in the United States. Most fundamentally, it refocused the politics of taxation on the progressive income tax and greatly raised the stakes of tax politics. On the one hand, taxation for World War I demonstrated the great revenue potential of progressive income taxation, even when it reached only the wealthiest Americans. The key components of nineteenth-century taxes—tariffs and sin taxes—paled in comparison as revenue machines. On the other hand, the scale of wartime taxation increased the capacity of the progressive income tax to redistribute wealth. As a consequence, the intensity of class and party conflict over taxation intensified sharply. The congressional elections of 1918 and the presidential election of 1920 were especially polarizing.

During these campaigns, the investment banking community, increasingly exercised over the excess-profits tax, and the leadership of the Republican Party seized on the popular concern with inflation and blamed the wartime tax program for causing it. This campaign helped turn the Democrats out of power and won popular support for the repeal of the excess-profits tax in 1921 and of significant tax cuts in individual rates. Other cuts followed during the 1920s and by 1928, Republicans had reduced the top marginal rate from 73 to 25 percent. This postwar reaction marked the beginning of periodic assaults by the Republican Party on progressive income taxation. At the same time, the Democrats dug in behind their "ability to pay" ideology, believing that it continued to have substantial public appeal.

The progressive income tax survived the class and partisan contests of the postwar period. A crucial reason for its survival was the emergence of a kind of enlightened self-interest on the part of key leaders of the Republican Party. Most important, Andrew Mellon, Secretary of the Treasury from 1921 to 1932, pragmatically supported preserving the progressive income tax, and even supported a preferential rate of taxation for earned income (wages and salaries) versus so-called "unearned" income (profits, capital gains, interest, and rents). He had several reasons for this. First, he appreciated the enormous revenue capacity of the progressive income tax and saw major economic benefits from the expansion of the federal government, which took place in the realms of national defense, highway construction, public lands and national parks, education, hydroelectric projects, the regulation of immigration and commerce, and the enforcement of Prohibition. Second, Mellon believed that embracing the ideology of "ability to pay" demonstrated the civic responsibility of Republicans. This would, he hoped, advance their electoral strength and defuse radical attacks on capital. Third, he had significant success in working with the tax-writing committees of Congress in order to create zones of privilege within the income tax code for particular industries, certain types of investments, and specific forms of income as well as for earned income. For example, the Revenue Act of 1921 introduced preferential rate of taxation for capital gains, setting it at the very low rate of 12.5 percent. (Later legislation tended to exclude portions of capital gains from income taxation.) While accepting the principle of "ability to pay," he introduced tax expenditures— exemptions and deductions—that partially offset the effects of the high marginal tax rates that had created powerful economic incentives for carving loopholes in the income tax code.

To justify this kind of tax reform, Mellon transformed the ideological content of tax politics. Throughout his long reign as Secretary of the Treasury, and especially in his 1924 book, *The People's Business*, Mellon outlined an alternative ideology to "ability to pay." He wrote that "the prosperity of the middle and lower classes depended upon the good fortunes and light taxes of the rich." High progressive taxation threatened to create powerful barriers to work, saving, and investment, Mellon warned, and while embracing the "ability to pay" standard, he also proposed removing the barriers to productive behavior. Much later, in 1961, Louis Eisenstein, a tax lawyer and scholar, famously described Mellon's alternative to the "ability to pay" ideology as the ideology of "barriers and deterrents."[4] Mellon's alternative ideology—or criterion, if you like—lent no more precision to the formulation of tax policy than had "ability to pay." Both criteria were little more than platitudes, slogans, or dogmas, offering little guidance to policymakers. This was unfortunate but at the same time it made it intellectually easier for Mellon, his supporters, and his political successors to embrace both "ability to pay" and what became known as "trickle-down" economics. Mellon argued that the creation of incentives within the tax code was sometimes necessary to promote socially desirable saving and investment—incentives that might depart from a simplistic application of "ability to pay." Popularizing such arguments helped legitimize the insertion of special exemptions or deductions into the income tax code, and the awarding of tax benefits to some groups or individuals made it easier for other groups or individuals to claim comparable benefits. From Mellon's time in the 1920s to the present day, the ideological contest over tax policy has been primarily one between variants of the "ability to pay" arguments, on the one hand, and variants of Mellon's "barriers and incentives" claims, on the other. These competing ideologies, whose operational definitions remain extremely vague, encourage a reform process that often includes "soak the rich" initiatives and special treatment for individuals and groups at the same time. In effect, Mellon fostered the development of a political middle-of-the-road path that simultaneously embraced the "ability to pay" and "trickle-down" approaches.

A major cost of this pragmatic resolution of competing ideologies and what might be reasonably called class interests was the loss of intellectual coherence in the operational definition of the central element of the tax base—the incomes of individuals. At the end of World War I, despite the expansion and elaboration of the income tax during the five stressful years since its introduction, the definition of an individual income never, before or since, conformed more closely to both economic and accounting definitions of income. In 1921, Robert Murray Haig, a public finance economist at Columbia, who during World War I had become a leading expert on income taxation throughout the world, declared that the concept of taxable income "as it stands in our own law is probably the closest approach to true economic income yet achieved by any country." The intellectual basis for Haig's judgment was the theoretical definition of income he had posed. "Income," he wrote, "is the money-value of the net accretion to economic power between two points in time."[5] In more familiar terms, income in Haig's definition included income from the factors of production of labor, land, and capital and increases in the value of land and capital. Haig's definition quickly carried the day within the field of public finance, and, refined during the 1940s by Herbert Simons, an economist at the University of Chicago, became known as "Haig-Simons" income taxation. Haig favored some degree of progressive taxation, but he did not have dogmatic views on the extent of progressivity desirable. But he was firm in his belief that the income and capital gains base of income taxation ought to be as broad as possible, insuring that gains in economic power ought to be taxed equally. Equals in economic power, in Haig's formulation, ought to be taxed equally. This standard was that of horizontal equity—horizontal fairness—as distinct from vertical equity, or greater progressivity. By 1924, economists who shared Haig's analytical and ethical perspectives grew critical of the income tax as defined by Andrew Mellon. The leader of this charge was Thomas S. Adams, a public finance economist at both the University of Wisconsin and Yale. He charged that the Mellon plan contained "incurable inequalities and inconsistencies." More generally, Adams concluded that the income tax was "not merely defective." It had, he wrote, "reached a condition of inequality the gravity of which could scarcely be exaggerated." The tax base had become so irrational, Adams concluded, that he was ready to abandon income taxation altogether. He proposed replacing it with a progressive tax on consumption rather than income—an idea that retains theoretical appeal today even though its implementation would face great political and administrative challenges. However, acceptance of Haig's reform made little headway until sixty years later.[6]

The next national emergency—the Great Depression—revived the progressive income tax as a dynamic source of revenue and generated popular support for tax reformers who wanted to advance an "ability to pay" program. The combination of weak federal revenues and expansive spending programs launched by presidents Herbert Hoover and Franklin Roosevelt led to bipartisan interest in increasing the capacity of the income tax. During Hoover's administration, bipartisan support enacted the Revenue Act of 1932, which imposed the largest peacetime tax increases in the nation's history. Most of the revenue it raised came from increasing personal and corporate income-tax rates across the board and reducing income-tax exemptions. The top marginal rate increased from 25 to 63 percent, thus returning to about World War I levels. Democrats welcomed the move toward "ability to pay" as well as toward deficit reduction. Further increases in progressive income taxation during Roosevelt's New Deal raised the rates on the wealthiest Americans: The effective rates on the richest one percent reached over 16 percent—a level higher than any year since World War I.[7] The most radical reform was the adoption in 1936 of a graduated tax on corporate profits that had not been distributed to stockholders. The New Deal modeled this tax, which it hoped would enhance competition by assaulting monopoly profits, on the excess-profits tax of World War I. This sent shudders through corporate boardrooms. A severe recession in 1937 to 1938 threatened to return the nation to the dark days of 1933, and a coalition of Republicans and conservative Democrats succeeded in blaming the New Deal's tax program for it. This coalition halted the reform program and succeeded in eradicating the excess-profits tax.

Yet another national crisis—the third major national crisis in the unstable first half of the twentieth century—stimulated another wave of tax reform. In fact, every significant national crisis in American history—war (the Revolution, the Civil War, the two world wars) and the Great Depression—has been accompanied by new tax regimes, systems of taxation with their own characteristic tax bases, rate structures, administrative set-ups, and social purposes.[8] The staggering costs of mobilizing for World War II, coupled with intense fears of inflation, called for far greater revenues than even World War I had demanded. Fortunately for the successful prosecution of the war, practical options had changed in several major ways. First, the obvious fighting strength of the enemies of the United States, and the early defeat at Pearl Harbor, contributed to an upsurge in patriotism, a spirit of sacrifice, and a willingness to comply voluntarily with an aggressive program of direct taxation. Second, the growth of the power of the federal government, particularly in the realm of public relations, reinforced the effectiveness of the government's call for sacrifice in the form of taxation as well as military service, rationing, and the purchase of war bonds. Third, the introduction of Social Security provided the means for the federal government to discover the identities of potential taxpayers. These three developments enabled the federal government to assess and collect income tax revenues from a large swath of the middle class. There is much truth to what many historians have claimed: With World War II the income tax shifted from a "class tax" to a "mass tax." The number of individual taxpayers grew from 3.9 million in 1939 to 42.6 million in 1945, and federal income-tax collections leapt from $2.3 billion to $35.1 billion, accounting for more than two-thirds of all federal tax revenues. By the end of the war, nearly 90 percent of the labor force submitted income-tax returns, and about 60 percent of the labor force paid income taxes.

While historians have often emphasized the new "mass tax" quality of the reformed income tax, the World War II tax retained many of its class tax elements. General deductions (for example, for interest on home mortgages and payments of state and local taxes) sweetened the new tax system for the middle-class. And, middle-class taxpayers preferred the mass-based income taxation to national sales taxation, which many corporate leaders favored and promoted. Most important, wartime revenue acts increased the marginal rates of taxation to levels ranging from 50 to more than 90 percent throughout the war. By 1944, the substantially higher marginal rates, coupled with wartime inflation, produced an effective rate on the richest one percent of Americans of 60 percent—an all-time high, and almost four times the highest level achieved during World War I.[9] Even with the broader base of taxation, the wealthiest one percent of households accounted for about one-third of all revenues under the personal income tax.

During the first 30 years of the modern U.S. income tax's existence, roughly its first generation, politicians engaged in sharp-edged contests over the tax, with uncertain results. Throughout this period American society was wracked by recurrent national crises, and the income tax—the tax system in general—seemed "up for grabs." In contrast, over the next generation, the period from World War II into the 1970s, the intensity of tax politics, especially its class dimensions, eased significantly. Various elements contributed to the subsiding passions.

The income tax continued to demonstrate its enormous capability to generate revenues, particularly in an environment of economic growth (which was sustained throughout its second generation), and in an economy prone to inflation (which was significant during the late 1940s and much of the 1960s and early 1970s). These revenues formed a significant element in what some fiscal historians have called "the era of easy finance."[10] I would rephrase that now as "the generation of easy finance." From the late 1940s into the 1970s these revenues funded programs that received bipartisan support—for example, national defense during the Cold War, the G.I. bill for benefits to World War II veterans, the Medicare entitlement program, and a wide range of discretionary domestic programs in the areas of education, health services, urban renewal, and infrastructure building. The federal government was able to fund these programs without increasing taxes and, in fact, while enacting major tax cuts—beginning in 1945 during the Truman administration and continuing through the administrations of Dwight D. Eisenhower (in 1954) and Lyndon Johnson (the Kennedy-Johnson tax cut of 1964), culminating in the Economic Recovery Tax Act (ERTA) of 1981, during the first year of the Reagan presidency. This act slashed rates across the full spectrum of income taxation and increased tax breaks that favored investments in capital-intensive industries. During this second generation, almost complete freedom from tax increases coupled with frequent, and popular, tax cutting became central elements in the continued political success of the income tax. At the same time, however, the reliance on invisible, or nearly invisible, sources of revenue and on tax cutting as a kind of welfare program for the beneficiaries of the cuts had weakened tax consent by weakening the connections that people saw between the taxes they paid and the government programs they valued.

The income tax system created in World War II continued to command popular support because of its embodiment of the "ability to pay" principle. But while Democratic politicians continued to invoke the slogan, they did so in a more restrained way. While they were slow to support large cuts in the top marginal rates, they took advantage of the vagueness of the "ability to pay" principle, and weak public understanding of the tax code, to reduce significantly the effective rates of taxation on the nation's richest citizens and corporations and broaden their political appeal to wealthier Americans. During the 1950s, bipartisan cutting of taxes through rate reductions and, more important, increases in tax exclusions, exemptions, and deductions, the effective rates on the wealthiest one percent of Americans decreased by more than half—from about 60 percent during the war to about 25 percent.

In advancing widely popular tax cuts, both Democrats and Republicans defended them with reference to two principles—one old, but refined, and one relatively new. The old principle was the supply-side or trickle-down idea championed by Andrew Mellon during the 1920s—the idea that cuts could stimulate greater effort by both workers and owners of capital and thus produce gains in productivity and levels of output. In the 1970s and 1980s, economists helped strengthen one aspect of this argument by pointing out that income taxation tended to favor consumption over investment. The argument was that while income taxation taxed every dollar of income consumed only once—that is, when it was received—it taxed every dollar of income saved multiple times, first when received and then again every time it produced additional income in the form of rent, interest, or profits. Calls for equalization of the playing field—an adaptation of tax fairness clichés— became the mantras of proponents of tax cuts designed to promote savings and capital formation. The relatively new argument was one that embraced the Keynesian counter-cyclical theories that had gained support from economists, many business representatives, and the general public from the late 1930s throughout the 1940s. Architects of the Kennedy-Johnson tax cuts in 1964 and even Reagan's 1981 tax cut often embraced the Keynesian idea that tax cuts as well as spending increases could support weak demand and thereby help offset downturns in the business cycle.

The most recent generation of income taxation began roughly in the late 1970s or early 1980s. The initiation of this phase came in the late 1970s with the slowing of long-term economic growth and the onset of more frequent recessions. Both weakened the economic base for income taxation. Also shaping this generation was the cumulative effect of the previous generation's tax cuts. In a way, the last act of the second generation of income taxation was also the first act of the third generation. This last and first act was the Economic Recovery Act of 1981, enacted by a bipartisan coalition during the first year of the Reagan administration. It touched off the first major acceleration of deficit spending since World War II. Interest rates increased in response and threatened to worsen the economic stagnation. In 1994, conservative economist Herbert Stein called the 1981 tax cut, coupled with a massive increase in defense spending by the Reagan administration, as the "Big Budget Bang." He wrote that it "ballooned the deficit up to levels never seen before" and fiscal policy became "dominated by efforts to deal with the consequences of that event.[11]

In response to the weakening of the income base for taxation, the increase in military spending, continued pressure on entitlement spending in the form of Social Security and Medicare, and the deficit explosion, three successive administrations—those of Ronald Reagan, George H. W. Bush, and Bill Clinton—took two major fiscal steps: raising taxes significantly and stabilizing the growth in discretionary spending on domestic programs. This bipartisan string of presidents collectively enacted the largest string of peacetime hikes in income taxes since the New Deal. Reagan's increases took the form of base-broadening through the reduction of various deductions and exemptions in 1982, just one year after the 1981 tax cut, and again in 1984. Bush and Clinton each signed measures to increase the highest marginal rates on individual incomes. Bush reluctantly approved an increase from 28 percent to 31 percent, and Clinton enthusiastically supported a further increase to 39.6 percent. These tax increases— from Reagan's in 1982 to Clinton's in 1993—coupled with resumed economic expansion, allowed President Clinton to submit, in January 1998, the first balanced federal budget in three decades.

Another contributor to fiscal consolidation and stabilization was the bipartisan Tax Reform Act of 1986 that the Reagan administration adopted in the mid-1980s to stabilize the tax system, calm the waters of tax politics, and create a tax system that was economically more efficient. The basic framework for reform was the model that Robert Murray Haig had proposed more than seventy years earlier: income taxation that would be broad-based and horizontally equitable or fair if it taxed in an even-handed fashion all forms of income and capital gains. This act represented the most significant income tax reform since World War II. The Reagan administration became genuinely committed to the economic theory behind the Haig model and worked within it in a highly pragmatic fashion. Most important, the administration used its willingness to increase tax revenues through broadening the base of income taxation, and its willingness to increase the progressivity of the tax system for low-income families to bargain for reduction of the highest marginal rates of income taxation. On the one hand, the administration agreed to major reforms that Democratic leaders wanted. These included slashing tax breaks for business and investment; taxing capital gains at the same rate that the income tax applied to the highest income earners; taking millions of poorer Americans off the tax rolls; and expanding the Earned Income Tax Credit (by providing a major increase in the "negative" income tax for poorer Americans). In return, the Republicans won Democratic support for a dramatic reduction of the top marginal income tax rate from 50 to 28 percent. In any case, many Republicans, especially within the administration, agreed with the Democrats that the elimination of tax breaks and the full taxation of capital gains would promote economic efficiency, particularly when combined with cuts in the highest tax rates. Despite the reductions in the top marginal rate, the tax system remained just as progressive at the end of the Reagan administration as it had been at the outset, but the 1986 act had shifted the system significantly toward greater horizontal equity—that is, toward treating economic equals equally under the law. As a consequence, I believe, during the late 1980s and into the 1990s public confidence in the income tax increased, frustrating the efforts of Newt Gingrich, with his Contract for America, and others to replace the income with various forms of consumption taxation.[12]

During the 1990s, however, the administrations of George H. W. Bush and Bill Clinton retreated from the 1986 compact, with Bush calling for significant cuts in capital gains and Clinton stressing the need for a progressive redistribution of income taxation through both rate increases and middle-class tax breaks. During these two administrations, the two major parties drifted back into competition over who could offer special favors within the tax code. With his election in 2000, George W. Bush broke further from the compact by making highly selective tax cuts his highest priority for domestic policy. He began in March 2001 with more moderate cuts than Reagan had championed in 1981, but in 2003 he enacted more dramatic cuts, including the reduction of the top rate of taxation of capital gains from 39.6 percent to 15 percent and of dividends from 20 percent to 15 percent.

In the process, George W. Bush lumped together all of the possible arguments for tax cutting, including both conservative supply-side and Keynesian arguments for stimulating demand. In fairness to his administration, however, there may well have been a coherent plan: to move the nation toward the repeal of all taxes on capital income, thereby applying the income tax exclusively to wages, salaries, and rents. With additional reforms, the plan may have been to turn the remaining income tax into a tax on consumption. But Bush and his advisers never crafted a coherent, principled appeal to the public on behalf of this strategy.

These Bush tax cuts had two major effects. The first was a shift from what we call today the income tax toward a tax that would be more accurately described as one on a hybrid of income and consumption because of the cuts in the tax rates on capital gains and dividends. The second was an increase in budgetary deficits. Of course, driving the deficits upward as well were the wars against terrorism, the reconstructions of Iraq and Afghanistan, the addition of a major drug benefit to Medicare, the relentless upward demographic and economic pressure on entitlement spending, and the stimulus spending that Bush initiated after the "Great Recession" took hold in 2008. The desire to stimulate recovery from both the demand and supply sides led Congress to extend the Bush tax cuts for two years, until December 31, 2012, and then again, in early 2013, permanently for most of the cuts.

With the Bush tax cuts, the federal government initiated another cycle of tax cuts, budget deficits, national debt, and finally tax increases to bring deficits and debt under control. The end of the cycle—or, more likely, the beginning of the end—has been, once again, increases in income taxes—those that Congress enacted in 2013. Increases seem likely to continue if and when President Obama and the Congress resume cooperation on fiscal consolidation. What is less clear is whether future tax reform will encompass more than selective increases and move into something closer to fundamental tax reform. I am confident, however, that the income tax will survive. It has many shortcomings, but the administrative problems, economic costs, and political challenges of making a full transition to a full-scale consumption-based tax would be daunting. It is possible, however, that at some point in the reform process reformers may turn to value-added taxation as a supplement to income taxation or a partial replacement, perhaps of Social Security payroll taxation or the corporate income tax.

In striving to reform rather than to replace the income tax, the challenge for policymakers will be to rise above the turbulent history of the income tax during its first and the third generations. It remains to be seen whether reformers succeed in making the tax not only more progressive but also more economically efficient, fairer in a horizontal sense, and politically more stable. The history of the first hundred years of the tax suggests that the best way to advance that multi-faceted agenda of improving the quality of federal taxation is to focus on the pursuit of comprehensive and fundamental reform along the lines of the Reagan model—the Tax Reform Act of 1986—and the earlier model of Robert Murray Haig. In the debates over taxes, deficits, and debt, the American public will continue to be divided over the optimal overall size of government and its components, the relative role of the income tax in the nation's revenue system, and the degree of progressivity within the rate structure of the income tax. But I think it is reasonable to hope that a search for a bipartisan compromise over all those fundamental issues will eventually elevate the ideal of horizontal tax equity. I regard that ideal as far more coherent, far more capable of rigorous definition, and broader in its popular appeal as a standard of fairness than either progressive equity or the doctrine of "barriers and deterrents." Implementing the Haig framework (the Reagan framework of 1986) could create a fairer tax system, reduce the temperature of tax politics, enhance the economic efficiency of the tax system, reduce the fog of fiscal uncertainty that clouds economic decisions, and help us meet the nation's future social and economic challenges with fiscal responsibility.

Footnotes

1. The most influential nineteenth-century construction of the "ability to pay" criterion was that of Jeremy Bentham and John Stuart Mill, who proposed "equal sacrifice" as the basis for establishing tax equity. They posited that an

increment of additional tax represented less sacrifice for wealthy than for poorer taxpayers. For a suggestion of the influence on this idea in nineteenth-century America, see W. Elliot Brownlee, "Social Philosophy and Tax Regimes in the United States, 1763 to the Present," *Social Philosophy and Taxation* 23 (Summer 2006):12–13.

2. W. Wilson to F. M. Simmons, September 4, 1913 in Arthur S. Link et al, eds., *The Papers of Woodrow Wilson*, vol. 28, *1913* (Princeton, NJ: Princeton University Press, 1978), 254.

3. W. Elliot Brownlee, "Historical Perspective on U.S. Tax Policy Toward the Rich," in Joel B. Slemrod, ed., *Does Atlas Shrug? The Economic Consequences of Taxing the Rich* (New York and Cambridge, MA: Russell Sage Foundation and Harvard University Press, 2000), 45.

4. Louis Eisenstein, *The Ideologies of Taxation* (Cambridge, MA: Harvard University Press, 2010), 47–71. The book was originally published in 1961 by the Ronald Press Company.

5. Robert M. Haig, "The Concept of Income," in *The Federal Income Tax* (New York: Columbia University Press, 1921), 7.

6. For Adams' views, see Thomas S. Adams, "The Economic and Social Basis of Tax Reduction," *Proceedings of the American Academy of Political Science* 11(March 1924):24–34; "Mellon Plan Finds Champion and Foe," *New York Times*, April 16, 1924; and T. S. Adams to Senator James E. Watson, April 11, 1924, Papers of Thomas S. Adams, Sterling Library, Yale University.

7. Brownlee, "Historical Perspective on U.S. Tax Policy Toward the Rich," 51.

8. For an outline of the history of American tax regimes since 1789, see W. Elliot Brownlee, *Federal Taxation in America: A Short History* (Washington, D.C. and Cambridge, UK: The Wilson Center Press and Cambridge University Press, 2004), 1–9.

9. Ibid., 60–61.

10. See, for example, C. Eugene Steuerle, "Financing the American State at the Turn of the Century," in W. Elliot Brownlee, ed., *Funding the American State, 1941–1995* (Washington, D.C. and Cambridge, UK: Woodrow Wilson Center Press and Cambridge University Press, 1996), 416–17.

11. Herbert Stein, "The Fiscal Revolution in America, Part II: 1964–1994," in W. Elliot Brownlee, ed., *Funding the American State, 1941–1995*, 266.

12. For suggestions of the effects of the 1986 on tax progressivity and public opinion, see W. Elliot Brownlee and C. Eugene Steuerle, "Taxation," in *The Reagan Presidency: Pragmatic Conservatism and Its Legacies* (Lawrence: University Press of Kansas, 2003), 173–74, and Brownlee, *Federal Taxation in America: A Short History*, 180. For supporting polling data, see Andrea Louise Campbell, "What Americans Think of Taxes," in *The New Fiscal Sociology: Taxation in Comparative and Historical Perspective* (Cambridge, UK: Cambridge University Press, 2009), 65–66.

GEORGE GILDER

The Supply-Side Insight

I have just finished work on a new book called *Knowledge and Power*, which is a sequel to *Wealth and Poverty*. It is based on my twenty-year study of technology. I have written a series of books on the microchip, one titled *Life After Television* predicted the Internet in 1990—worldwide webs of glass and light—and *Telecosm*, and a series of books on technology. These books are based ultimately on a field of study called information theory.

Information theory sprung from computer science and communication science and networking science. The leading figure in information theory was a man named Claude Shannon, a professor at MIT and a major figure at Bell Labs. Claude Shannon had developed an elaborate mathematical system for calculating the capacity of any channel or circuit in a network, and his findings are the foundation for the information economy in which we live.

A few years ago I began to see that Shannon's theory solved a fundamental problem of capitalist economics. I had been studying economics for decades and it seemed to me that all the economic models that prevailed, virtually all of them, suffered from one crucial flaw—they could not truly explain or encompass entrepreneurial creativity. And yet, as all my books have said, "entrepreneurial creativity is the heart of economic growth." If you don't understand entrepreneurial creativity, economic growth will always elude your models. So all the various economic models failed to come to terms with the central fact of economic life, which is creativity, innovation, entrepreneurship, and human imagination.

The key factor in creativity is that it always comes as a surprise to us. If creativity wasn't surprising, we could predict it and plan it—and we wouldn't need it. And socialism would work. So the crux was that because creativity comes as a surprise, any economic model that is based on mimicking the determinist schemes of physics, which is what all economic models since the time of Adam Smith have attempted to do, will miss the surprises of entrepreneurial creativity. But information theory defines information as surprise. If you already know everything I tell you, I convey zero information—no suprises. That is why political speeches are so hopelessly boring most of the time. Politicians, or their speechwriters, try to determine by market surveys and polls and every other kind of exploration what their audience already thinks, already knows. Then they distill those views into some sort of rhetorical form. The results are the zero-information speeches that most politicians give. Most of our politicians won't assess our real predicaments and provide serious leadership. Leadership has to be created, it has to be surprising or it won't galvanize the people to follow and make the efforts that are necessary.

Peter Drucker said, "Don't solve problems," which, at first, seems a peculiar statement. Human beings get up in the morning and start solving problems. That is the predicament of our species. But Peter Drucker understood that when you solve problems you end up feeding your failures, starving your strengths, and achieving costly mediocrity. Don't solve problems was Peter Drucker's counsel—*pursue opportunities*. That is crucial to understand when in a desperate predicament such as we are today, where the overwhelming impulse is to keep digging. And you know the first law of holes.

While we are busy celebrating the centennial of the income tax, we should not leave out a few celebratory toasts to the other centennial of 2013—that of the Federal Reserve Bank, which, of course, supplies the punchbowl, the famous punchbowl, for the party. We should be grateful to the Fed. Indeed, it has been suggested that since the Fed exists, we shouldn't even be talking about the income tax. Why do we bother maintaining this elaborate apparatus of the IRS and the rest when the Fed can just print money? The current policy of the Fed is zero interest rates as far as the eye can see. In other words, free money.

However, whenever anything is free, it tends to get scarce quickly, and somehow only the privileged and advantaged manage to get any of it. Zero interest rates really mean that a few privileged banks with access to the Fed get the free money. They then turn around and lend that money to the Treasury and small businesses and job-creating entrepreneurs, those left out of the loop. Big corporations are overloaded with capital today. They leave trillions of dollars in Europe and elsewhere around the world rather than return it to the United States and face the hostile climate that currently exists here. These privileged banks are, however, heavily regulated, which means that the government determines the targets for capital; thus the entrepreneurial surprise that is critical to all economic growth is omitted from the scheme.

There is a great deal of this illusory "free" in this country. For example, we find it in Obamacare, which is really just a scheme for extracting ever more taxes from the American people. The key thing we know about it is that it entails hiring 16,000 more IRS agents. That is in the bill—16,000 more IRS agents. But at the same time, they are taxing the other parts of medicine, including the most creative parts—such as in the development of medical instruments—where entrepreneurial surprise might occur. New devices that may make our lives longer and more enjoyable are being taxed on a gross revenues tax, gross sales tax. A new company launching some sort of new medical device may have all of its profits taken by the gross sales tax. There are no provisions for more doctors or nurses in Obamacare, just more IRS agents, so what you have is a repetition of the same phenomenon we see with free money. Zero-interest rate policy, ZIRP, means that only the advantaged and privileged get access to the capital. Similarly that is what happens when you have free medical care: It is distributed according to queues, and the advantaged tend to have ways to get to the heads of those queues.

So knowledge and power get separated. The real insight of information theory is that capitalism is not chiefly an incentive system: It is an information and knowledge system. The reason capitalism works better than all other forms of economic organization is that the same people who conduct successful experiments of enterprise and investment are granted the right to continue the process. In other words, it is a learning process. Karl Popper explains that to have a learning experience, you really need to have a falsifiable experiment. That is an experiment that can be negated, that can fail. In business terms it means you have to permit bankruptcy. If you don't permit failure, it is not a capitalist venture: It is crony capitalism, it is trickle-down socialism, it is all kinds of things—but it is not capitalism if failure is prohibited by government power. If the government inserts its power to ordain outcomes, then knowledge does not accumulate, and knowledge in companies and entrepreneurial heads is the source of all increasing wealth and value. When you divorce knowledge from power as government does in this way, that is, depriving the entrepreneur of the income he needs to continue his process of falsifiable investment, enterprises that can fail, and thus teach lessons of failure as well as the lessons of success, don't fail. But the successful entrepreneurs get to continue the process because they have learned they are capable of creating evermore value.

Hillsdale College is living proof of this assertion. By refusing all government aid, all government guarantees, Hillsdale has made it possible for it to fail, and thus has made it possible for it to learn institutionally. It becomes a source of new creativity and imagination and knowledge in the economy. Colleges that allow themselves to be guaranteed by government are essentially deprived of this virtue. They don't create real knowledge. They indulge various social causes and professorial distractions, but they don't really create knowledge and if they did, you would have no way of knowing it. By repudiating government aid Hillsdale asserts the primacy of knowledge over federal power and the benefits of creativity over coercion and privilege.

Having this insight that capitalism is not chiefly an incentive system but a knowledge system is important to understanding taxation and its effects. As a supply sider, the great supply-side insight was the Laffer curve. The Laffer curve essentially showed that lower tax rates could yield more revenues than higher tax rates. Indeed there are two tax rates where zero revenues are received—a zero tax rate and a 100 percent tax rate. Somewhere in the middle of the curve is the optimal point where the most tax revenues are generated. The Laffer curve has been massively vindicated and demonstrated over the years since it was propounded. Many say that during the 2012 political campaign, the Congressional Research Service released a report that showed that tax hikes actually produce more economic growth than tax cuts. This was a remarkable finding. They found it by scrutinizing a few episodes of tax cuts and tax hikes over the last twenty years, mostly during the Clinton administration when, contrary to what many people imagine, tax rates were reduced significantly. A 30 percent cut in capital gains taxes and a 10 percent raise in personal income tax rates add up to a huge spur for entrepreneurial activity and creativity. Virtually all the increased revenues that did follow Clinton's tax policy came through the capital gains tax cut. Remember the prodigal options that were being generated all over Silicon Valley, and across the country, the huge boom in telecom, internet stocks, dotcoms? All this was the source of the Clinton administration's success in balancing the budget. It wasn't done by increasing the personal income tax by 10 percent. That had virtually no impact compared to the vast expansion of capital gains and real estate gains and wealth that occurred.

So now during the Obama administration, we face increases not only in income tax rates, and taxes on medical care, medical instruments, payroll tax increases, capital gains tax increases, dividend tax increases, a whole array across the spectrum of rising tax rates, we face the question of how to respond to this situation in the face of essentially 40 percent deficits every year. To understand the phrase "don't solve problems, pursue opportunities," it is worthwhile to compare the Carter administration with the Reagan administration. For example, Carter really did balance all governmental budgets, including state and local surpluses. Carter balanced the budget. Also, for the first time, he had a trade surplus. This signified capital flight because a trade surplus may mean that capital is leaving the country, and, indeed, under Carter there was capital flight from the United States. So although the government was in the black during the Carter administration, the private sector was in the red. We had runaway inflation and interest rates close to 20 percent and real double-digit unemployment—just all kinds of appalling economic conditions in the private sector—but the government was in the black. Then President Reagan assumed office and created a trillion dollars of new debt. This is regarded by some as providing a case against the Reagan administration compared to the Carter administration. Many think that Carter was more fiscally sound than Reagan. But while Reagan did add a trillion dollars to the deficit, at the same time most of that trillion dollars went to the defense budget, which was used to win the Cold War and so opened the communist world to capitalism for the first time. This was a tremendous breakthrough and triumph for the West. Meanwhile, he also touched the third rail of Social Security. He made an agreement with Tip O'Neil that restricted Social Security payments into the future, which constituted a $6 trillion improvement in the nation's liabilities that kept Social Security solvent for the subsequent twenty years. So while Reagan did increase the debt by a trillion dollars, at the same time he, with the Democrats, reduced Social Security liabilities by $6 trillion: That is a net gain of $5 trillion. Reagan also pursued other opportunities—tax rate reductions, deregulation, energy emancipation—that ended up allowing a $17 trillion increase in private sector assets. This launched a twenty-year boom that led to some $60 trillion of private sector assets.

So what do we learn from this? We learn that a focus on opportunities is more effective than a focus on liabilities. David Stockman, Reagan's budget director, cannot really tell the difference between Reagan and Carter, or Reagan and Obama: All he can see are liabilities, when what really matters are national assets. Our national debt is unsupportable because it is accompanied by policies that devalue our national assets.

Most economists tend to believe in the intractability of existing economic conditions, whether that is 1970s' inflation and stagflation or 2010s' deficits. But with a policy reversal you could transform the infoscape in a way that could transform the country overnight. Supply siders don't focus on this because we tend to stress tax rates. Tax rates remained very high after the Second World War, and we have allowed liberal economists to claim that the postwar economic boom was a result of the 91 percent tax rates in place at that time. The post-World War II era was one of the most important times in the history of the American economy: I believe that economy saved the West. What made that possible was the massive Republican sweep in the congressional elections of 1946. At the time Republicans planned to cut government spending not by 10 or 20 percent or even by 50 percent: The Republicans planned to cut government spending by 60 percent! Many of these cuts were in defense spending, but, nonetheless, there was a 61 percent reduction in government spending after the Second World War. Contemplating this effect, the Keynesian economists from Hanson to Samuelson predicted total catastrophe. Samuelson said, "This would be the worst dislocation and unemployment in the history of economics." This is how alarmed the Keynesian economists were.

These economists believed that a drastic drop in government spending would be catastrophic for the economy. Indeed, government spending went from 42 percent of GDP to 14 percent of GDP at the time. Not only did the Republicans cut government spending, they dismantled the entire New Deal regulatory and wartime structure. The WPA, the War Production Board, the War Labor Board, the Office of Price Administration—150,000 civilian government regulators and about one million government employees were laid off. The result—as Nobel laureate Paul Krugman, who epitomizes the dominant school of liberal big-spending economists today, points out—was a catastrophe and vindicated Keynesian economics because in 1946 there was a 20.6 percent drop in measured GDP. However, that instantly ignited a transformative surge of economic growth that continued for a decade and made the U.S. the world's leading economy. It allowed the U.S. to launch the Marshall Plan, which retrieved, and provided an example for, the war-devastated European economies. I think it is a mistake that supply-side economists don't focus more on this. As you might expect with a 61 percent drop in government spending, there were large tax rate reductions. One such reduction was in the joint income tax, which was created effectively since families remained intact at that point: It amounted to a 50 percent reduction in tax exposure for most American households. There were drastic corporate tax reductions. And nobody paid taxes in the 91 or 86 percent rates. I think there were 127 tax returns at those rates.

There are examples of this all around the world. New Zealand essentially zeroed out its government and moved from one of the least successful economies in the world to one of the most. Today it has the single best business climate in the world according to some sources. I wrote about the Israeli economy in *Israel Test*: When the environment is changed to an information system, it is dominated by knowledge, not power. Policy changes in the knowledge domain can galvanize the material economy and transform it, while all the government TARPs and stimuli in the world can do nothing because they destroy knowledge and information rather than enhance it.

Don't solve problems, pursue opportunities—and there are huge opportunities to purse. There is no reason the U.S. economy cannot be completely turned around with a massive change of regime over the next decade.

DANIEL J. MITCHELL

The Case for the Flat Tax

Although I am about to state the case for the flat tax, I would like to go back to what our Founding Fathers had in mind: a very small central government that doesn't require any broad-based tax whatsoever. That said, and understanding that my fantasies won't be met right away, I do support the flat tax as a transitional financing mechanism until we reach the promised land of limited government.

As an economist, I can give you some context for why tax reform is important.

First, what are the two factors of production? Capital and labor. It persumably doesn't matter whether you are Paul Krugman, Karl Marx, or Milton Friedman—any economist should say the same thing. The only way to get more economic output is by providing more labor to the economy, more capital to the economy, or by using your labor and capital more efficiently. Who performs that role? The entrepreneur. (In the previous essay, you read what George Gilder wrote about the role of entrepreneurs, people who mix capital and labor together.)

Entrepreneurship, which occurs in the private sector, is a learning process. The role of the entrepreneur is to figure out what satisfies consumer needs and to put capital and labor together in ways that meet those needs in a profitable manner. Profits—as well as losses—play a key role. These "bottom line" numbers are a signal to entrepreneurs, and this ongoing process of learning how to profitably and efficiently utilize resources is what generates economic growth.

Government may try to play the same role, but without the feedback process. The result is that people in the private sector who figure out good ways to deliver products and services to consumers are rewarded; the government, by contrast, tends to reward the bad ways of doing things.

Let's remind ourselves why growth matters. Does it matter whether you grow 2 percent a year or 3 percent a year? In our weak current recovery, economic growth has been far below normal standards. Usually after a recession, we bounce back with several years of 4 or 5 percent growth. Now we are struggling simply to get back to the long-run average of 3 percent growth. Does this matter?

Imagine that an economy grows 1 percent a year. It takes that economy 70 years to double its GDP. Compare that to a high-growth economy: Even at 4 percent a year, it doubles its GDP in fewer than 20 years. At 7 percent growth, it doubles in ten years. So growth rate matters a lot. A 0.2-percent increase in an economic growth rate in the U.S. economy would mean the difference, after 25 years, of more than $4,000 for the average household.

Since economic growth is so critical, we need to figure out how we can encourage it—or at the least, determine how to remove the impediments government has created—so that entrepreneurs have the ability to utilize labor and capital in ways that make us more prosperous.

Before I delve into taxes, let me give you another caveat. My first caveat was that I don't really want the flat tax: I want a very small government and no broad-based tax. The second caveat is that it is important to realize that taxes are just one of many government policies that affect economic growth. If you look at the *Economic Freedom of the World* indexes put out by the Fraser Institute, the Cato Institute, and other think tanks around the world, you see that five major factors of economic growth are graded: (1) rule of law and property rights, (2) monetary policy, (3) regulatory policy, (4) trade policy, and (5) fiscal policy.

In the index, fiscal policy is only 20 percent of a nation's grade, and that includes spending and taxes. Assuming they are weighted equally, that means taxes are only 10 percent of a nation's grade. So a nation's economic performance will depend on many things, with taxes being one small part of the equation.

Consider Ukraine: It has a flat tax, but almost every other government policy is very statist, very interventionist, and very corrupt. Consequently Ukraine doesn't have much economic growth. So while the flat tax can be used as a transitional financing mechanism until we achieve the goal of small government, it is not a silver bullet. You have to do other things right, as well. Government spending, for example, is critically important.

Even with a good tax system in place, if a government has expanded beyond its legitimate functions—if it becomes too big, too bloated, too inefficient—the end results will not be good. Sweden is an example of this. Sweden's tax system is actually very good on a per-krona-raised basis. But because the burden of government spending consumes almost 50 percent of its GDP, Sweden has—in the aggregate—a very onerous tax system. Sweden could take the extra step and institute a flat tax, but it would have to be a flat tax like the one Iceland used to have, which was about 37 percent. There is very little point in having a flat tax if it is going to be that high.

In other words, it is difficult to have a good tax system when government spending is out of control.

That is a problem we face in America. Government spending doubled during the Bush and Obama years. I put them together intentionally because both administrations are big spenders. This is really bad news for the future. If we don't want America to suffer from the economic problems afflicting Europe—such as stagnation, high youth unemployment, etc.—we had better figure out how to get government under control and put a good tax system in place. Right now the trend lines are not good at all.

What constitutes a good tax policy? There are a handful of simple rules: Tax at a low rate, tax income only once, tax all incomes alike, and tax on a territorial basis.

Why would we want a low marginal tax rate? A low marginal tax rate is the price a government imposes on whatever is being taxed. Politicians actually understand this—when they want to. How many times have we seen a politician bang his fist on the table, saying, "We want higher taxes on tobacco because we want people to smoke less"? While I don't like government trying to control people's lives, I give them an A-plus for economics. They understand that the more you tax something, the less you get of it. What frustrates me about our legislators in Washington is that they forget that elementary microeconomic lesson when it comes to taxes on work, saving, investment, risk taking, and entrepreneurship.

We should want tax rates as low as possible on the things that create wealth, prosperity, and competitiveness for our economy. Moreover, when tax rates are low, people are more likely to comply with the tax system. This is one of the reasons compliance with the tax system is so low in Greece. (That and the fact that Greece has a corrupt, inefficient government.) By contrast, where there is a very low tax rate and an honest efficient government, such as you find in Singapore and Switzerland, there is virtually no tax evasion and virtually no tax avoidance. Academic research indicates that at rates of 20 percent or below, people are willing, by and large, to comply with the tax system. Even if you don't approve of what the government is doing, a 20 percent tax rate is basically accepted as a cost of doing business.

What about double taxation? Every economic theory that I am aware of agrees that you cannot have economic growth unless you have capital formation—that is, saving and investing. You can't have prosperity tomorrow unless you set aside some of your income today.

But as this example illustrates, people who save and invest are mistreated. Let's say you have some income. You pay tax on that income, which leaves you with after-tax earnings. There are only two things you can do with those after-tax earnings: You can save and invest them or you can consume them. (Or you could say that you can either consume that after-tax income today or you can consume that after-tax income in the future, which is, of course, the same as savings and investment.)

If you spend your after-tax earnings immediately—maybe you buy a big screen TV—the federal government leaves you alone (although you may pay a state or local sales tax). But what if you do the responsible thing for yourself and society? What if you do what every economic theory says is the right thing for economic growth? What if you save and invest? With what is now a 23.8 percent capital gains tax, a 35 percent corporate tax, a 23.8 percent maximum tax double tax on dividends, and a 40 percent death tax, income that is saved and invested may be taxed as many as four times (and you still pay state and local sales tax when you buy the big screen TV in the future).

Now I'm not a rocket scientist, but if I walk down street A and everyone leaves me alone, but if I walk down street B it is likely someone will hit me over the head with a two-by-four, I am definitely being encouraged to walk down street A. To be blunt, I am being encouraged by our current tax structure to not save and invest: I am encouraged to consume. There are always politicians in Washington who say, "The American people are too short-sighted, they don't save enough." These politicians don't seem to realize that bad tax policy is a big reason we don't save enough. Policies from Washington punish the people who do save and invest. This is a very misguided economic policy.

What about loopholes, deductions, credits, exemptions, preferences, and exclusions? When government seeks to change our behavior with the tax code, it is industrial policy. It is the government trying to encourage us to make decisions on the basis of what they have put into the 74,000 pages of U.S. tax law and regulation: But picking winners and losers does not makes economic sense. That is very inefficient, it doesn't matter whether the government spends the money directly or it simply lays a trail of breadcrumbs to lure us into spending the money. If we are making decisions directly or indirectly, and we are doing things that are inefficient because of the government, that is going to hurt our economy and hurt our efficiency.

So while we do want to get rid of loopholes, such as tax shelters, we also need to make sure we define the tax base correctly so that we get rid of double taxation. We also want a territorial tax system. While not terribly important for purposes of this discussion, this simple concept says if something happens inside the U.S., the U.S. should tax it; if something happens inside Germany, Germany should tax it, and so forth. This is a big issue only if you care about international tax competition, which is one of my favorite issues. Suffice it to say that if people want to move their money to Switzerland, at that point it is not the U.S. federal government's business, it is the Swiss government's business.

What we have talked about here—low rate, no double taxation, no loopholes—that is the flat tax: It is territorial. It is a simple post-card-based system. The form that the Army-Shelby people showed to illustrate their flat tax plan in the 1990s was ten lines long. It was so simple it could fit on the back of a postcard.Go to the IRS Web site and compare that simple form to the more than one thousand forms and publications you can download at irs.gov.

Our tax code could have the simplicity of a flat tax. All you would need to know, under a flat tax, is your wage and salary income and the size of your family. (Maybe some of the politicians in Washington don't know how many kids they have, but most of us do.)

For businesses it could be just as simple. Start with the gross receipts from sales, subtract the wages paid to employees, the costs of raw materials, and any investment expenditures. Then apply the appropriate tax rate to what is left and—that's it.

Now, of course, simplicity isn't always a virtue. There are rumors that Barack Obama is going to introduce a two-line tax reform: (1) What did you make last year? (2) Send it to the IRS.

The good news is the flat tax concept is picking up steam around the world. When I first came to Washington, in the 1980s, there were only three flat-tax jurisdictions worldwide: Now there are more than thirty. The flat tax has completely swept much of the former Soviet empire: Russia has a flat tax, as does Estonia and Mongolia. Hong Kong has a very successful flat-tax system.

Time for another important caveat: None of the flat-tax juris-dictions—even the very good ones such as they have in Hong Kong, Estonia, and Georgia—have the ideal system proposed by Alvin Rabushka and Robert Hall more than thirty years ago. Many of the existing systems simply took the old tax code and imposed one rate on it. If all the deductions and other complications remain in place, you are not making major progress.

But some nations did make big leaps in the right direction. A few years ago I was in Bratislava, Slovakia, giving a presentation on tax reform at the Economics University. When I mentioned our (at the time) 72,000-page tax code, another professor on the panel reached into her briefcase and pulled out something that looked like a maga-zine. "This," she said, "is our tax code. Our entire tax code. Our VAT, our payroll tax, our excise taxes, our corporate income tax. And our flat tax system." As I recall, the flat tax portion was nineteen pages long. The bad news is that in 2013 the new socialist government of Slovakia got rid of the flat tax. The good news is that the jurisdictions that still have good flat tax systems, like those of Estonia and Hong Kong, are growing rapidly and doing very well.

What about opposition? There are really two arguments against the flat tax. Inside the Beltway, this is an issue of special interest groups, a political power game. It's almost as if every one of those 74,000 pages in our tax code benefits some specific group that will fight to retain the status quo.

Outside the Beltway, it is an issue of class warfare. Some people on the left think that the economy is a fixed pie; that if someone like Bill Gates gets a big slice of pie, then by definition, the rest of us must be worse off. If you have the mentality that America is a zero sum society, then you are, of course, upset by a tax system that makes it possible for someone who is rich on paper to receive a tax cut because you think that his gain comes at your expense.

That mindset is completely wrong, but I have found that this attitude is one of our biggest challenges. The average person doesn't understand that over time economic growth means that everyone will be better off. As JFK said, "the rising tide does lift all boats." We have to explain why it is important to have upward mobility and economic expansion. We are not doing a good enough job at that key task.

And, of course, most people don't understand capital formation and its relationship to rising living standards.

The flat tax means no double taxation, which means no capital gains tax, no death tax, nothing that penalizes saving and investment. Some people think that this means Warren Buffet, for example, does not pay tax. Of course he does! His income is being taxed at the corporate level: We just don't want to double and triple and quadruple tax it.

What we have before us is an educational mission. We must try to convince and educate people. Right now, we are not doing a good enough job. Our basic message is that we want growth, not redistribution; that we can help the poor climb out of poverty with an economic system that promotes prosperity. Winston Churchill once said, "the inherent vice of capitalism is the unequal sharing of blessings; the inherent virtue of socialism is the equal sharing of miseries."[1]

The flat tax is more than a one-tax rate system. The goal is to have low marginal tax rates: that is what determines people's incentives to engage in productive behavior. Iceland's old system notwithstanding, if we look around the world, flat-tax jurisdictions have low marginal tax rates. But why a 15 percent rate instead of a system with rates of 13 percent and 17 percent? I think there is a moral argument for a single rate. It is etched above the main entrance to the Supreme Court building—"Equal Justice under Law." Why on earth wouldn't we want that as an economic system? If you are applying for a license to run a business, the rules don't differ depending on your income. If you commit a crime, the punishment shouldn't be based upon your net worth. Throughout our economic system we understand that the rule of law means that people are treated equally—until it comes to taxation. There we discriminate as a deliberate and explicit matter of public policy. That is morally wrong.

It also undermines taxpayer unity. We recently witnessed the "fiscal cliff" debate in Washington, which ended with a tax increase that punishes those who contribute the most to the nation's wealth.

This happened, at least in part, because the politicians had the ability to play a divide-and-conquer game.

Imagine, however, if the United States were more like Massachusetts. Now in general, I don't want the U.S. to be more like Massachusetts, but in this case it is a useful example. Massachusetts, by a quirk in its state constitution, has a flat tax. And you better believe the big spenders in Massachusetts hate that flat tax. They have tried several times to change that law, but it can only be done by the vote of the people. The last time it was tried, which was the fourth or fifth attempt, was in 1994, the year Ted Kennedy was reelected in a landslide. The special interest groups were very clever. They designed their flat-tax repeal referendum so that about 90 percent of Massachusetts voters—in theory—would get a tax cut. "Vote for this referendum," the voters were told, "and you'll get a tax cut! And we will make those evil bad rich people pay more."

By a margin of about 2 to 1, the Massachusetts voters saw through that ruse. They realized that once they gave the politicians the ability to tax one group of people at a higher tax rate, it was only a matter of time before they taxed all people at a higher rate.

In other words, taxpayers are naturally united against the political class in a one-rate system.

There is also an administrative argument. I mentioned earlier the flat-tax postcard, which taxes only wage and salary income. All capital income is taxed on the business postcard. Administratively you can do that because in effect you have a withholding tax on capital income. This gets a little bit into boring economic terms, but "taxing at the source" means the government does not need to track down everyone's assets; the IRS doesn't need to track down who has interest, who owns stocks; and the government doesn't need to worry about transfers of wealth upon death. The flat tax is not only good economically, it is also good for privacy because the government never needs to know about your personal holdings. I think that is a virtue. Some in Washington think that is a bad thing.

Other tax reform options are examined within this book, for example, the national sales tax. I testified to Congress in favor of the national sales tax. I have debated in favor of the national sales tax. I have spoken on television in favor of the national sales tax. The national sales tax, the value-added tax, the inflow-outflow tax—there are many different types of tax systems that could fulfill or satisfy the principles I addressed at the beginning: that is, a low tax rate, no double taxation, and no loopholes. While I like the idea of a national sales tax, what I don't like—what I absolutely hate—is the possibility that something like a value-added tax be added to our current system on top of the income tax. It is theoretically an acceptable replacement tax. But if it is an add-on tax, it becomes a money machine for big government. At that point, start looking for property in Australia because you will know we are on an express train to becoming Greece.

What are the conditions for instituting a national sales tax? One condition has to be not only the repeal of the Sixteenth Amendment, but its replacement with something so ironclad even Chief Justice John Roberts wouldn't be able to rationalize that an income tax is constitutional again.

Keep in mind that the 1895 case *Pollock v. Farmers' Loan & Trust Company*, which ruled income tax unconstitutional, was decided by a five-to-four margin—and that was back when justices actually cared about what was in the Constitution. If all we did was to repeal the Sixteenth Amendment and politicians tried to keep the income tax, I have no faith that today's Supreme Court justices would vote the right way.

By the way, the temporary Civil War income tax (which presumably survived legal challenges) was a 3-percent flat tax. The 1894 income tax that was ruled unconstitutional in 1895 was a 2-percent flat tax. So the United States actually has a history of flat taxation.

With this bit of legal history to guide us, you can see why many experts think that the national sales tax is a good idea only if you put the Sixteenth Amendment six feet under the ground, in a lead-lined vault, with six feet of concrete over it, and then covered with a foot of salt so nothing can spring up again.

If that happens, then the sales tax is just as attractive as the flat tax. Why? Because they are different sides of the same coin. The flat tax taxes your income when you earn it—one time at one low rate. The sales tax taxes your income when you spend it—one time at one low rate.

They are economically identical plans, and they both have ways to protect the poor from taxation. The flat tax includes a generous personal allowance, while the sales tax has a "prebate," which basically offsets the sales tax on purchases up to the poverty level. They are basically the same plan. And that is good. It is also good that we are arguing about how best to fix our corrupt, inefficient, punitive tax system.

But the problem is that we are having this debate amongst ourselves. How do we get the crowd in Washington to go along with us? This is a big problem because politicians love class warfare, they love using the tax code to raise campaign cash. Despite the fact that the empirical evidence is on our side, even though we can see how quickly flat-tax countries like Hong Kong are growing, and how slowly class-warfare countries like France are growing, politicians love to spend money, they love to demonize the rich. Why on earth would these politicians ever fix the problem?

Maybe there will be another Ronald Reagan in the White House. Or even another Bill Clinton. (He was the second most free-market president in the post-WW II era.) Unfortunately, we don't have those kinds of president very often. What about having more people like Phil Graham and Dick Armey in Congress? Again, that doesn't happen very often. Will we ever have a controlling majority of people who actually want to do what is right for the country? And if we do, remember Lord Acton's caution: "Power corrupts and absolute power corrupts absolutely." One thing I have learned in my 25-plus years in Washington: Newly elected officials arrive thinking Washington is a cesspool. After ten years, they think it's a hot tub.

I have already mentioned that I am a big fan of international tax competition. Why do we now have thirty flat-tax jurisdictions in the world, when previously there had been only three? The answer is that these countries are competing with each other. In this era of globalization it is very easy for labor and capital to cross national borders. And just as we see what happens when states compete—

businesses left California after it instituted a 13.3 percent tax rate and moved to zero-tax Nevada; overtaxed people in New York escaped to zero-income-tax Florida—the same thing happens internationally. Because there has been tax competition and globalization for over the last thirty years, top income tax rates have come down dramatically, corporate tax rates have come down dramatically, and we have seen a big upswing in the number of flat-tax jurisdictions.

So what is the bottom line? High tax rates discourage people from earning income. High tax rates discourage people from reporting income. The combination of the two means that if tax rates rise above a certain level, not as much revenue will be collected as predicted by "static" estimates. You may, in fact, lose revenue. The IRS publishes its Statistics of Income every year, and they are all available online. In 1980, when the tax rate was 70 percent, the statistics showed there were about 117,000 wealthy people in America, who had reported $36 billion in income to the IRS: Uncle Sam got $19 billion. By 1988, President Reagan had lowered the top tax rate to 28 percent. What happened to revenue? Did it fall proportionally to about $8.5 billion? Did revenues fall to $15 billion, implying that more than half of the revenue was made up for by additional economic growth? Did revenue stay at $19 billion dollars implying that this tax cut paid for itself? None of the above. Revenue went up. The 1988 Statistics of Income data showed that there were 724,000 wealthy people, who reported nearly ten times as much income as had been reported by the "rich" in 1980. Consequently, the government got five times as much revenue. True, we had 40 percent inflation during this period; we had a 7 to 8 percent population increase; other of Reagan's reforms likely resulted in an increase in the number of wealthy people with their increased taxable income. The other thing this shows is that the members of Congress who were fighting against Reagan in the 1980s—who said that the Reagan tax rate reduction was unfair, that it was going to starve the government of revenue—were wrong.

And they are still wrong today when they oppose tax reform.

Footnote

1. https://www.nationalchurchillmuseum.org/socialism-quotes.html.

The Case for the FairTax

In the 1990s, when I was in Congress, I was a co-sponsor of flat tax bills, back when Dick Armey was sponsoring the flat tax on a regular basis. But lately I have come to a different conclusion. I think we need to change directions.

The tax we have today—that you have come to know and love—is a flat tax on income...100 years later. We flattened it out in 1986 only to have it amended about 20,000 times since then.

The hope that future Congresses will leave the flat tax alone reminds us of that proverbial third marriage—the victory of hope over experience. It isn't going to happen.

As long as Congress knows how much you make and how you make it, they are going to try and get it.

I propose an approach in which the government has no idea how much you make and doesn't even care.

Under the current system in this country people in business make decisions for tax reasons rather than economic reasons. You've been there. You get up in the morning and want to take care of your employees, your customers, your shareholders. But sitting at the head of the table is the taxman with 72,000 pages of complications written by people who have never had a customer or an employee. Those decisions lead to inefficiencies that cost money.

The current circumstance leads us to a situation where the Tax Foundation says that we are currently spending between $350 and $400 billion every year just filling out IRS forms. It costs a typical small business $724 to collect, comply, and remit $100. That is not just inefficiency: That is stupid.

It has led to an underground economy of $2 to $3 trillion a year that contributes nothing to our government. Today we have offshore financial centers with dollar-denominated deposits of between $15 and $20 trillion. This money wants to be in our economy, but is offshore because of the tax consequences of repatriation. I once asked Alan Greenspan how long it would take for that offshore money to be returned to our markets, to our banks. He said months. Why are we continuing to drive that money away?

Today 22 percent of what you currently spend at retail outlets represents the embedded cost of the IRS. You are paying the income tax costs and the payroll tax costs and the accountants and the attorneys to avoid the tax costs of each of the thousands of companies it takes to get a loaf of bread to your table. From getting oil out of the ground to make gasoline to getting ore out of the ground to make steel.

All of those businesses have costs. They have labor costs and travel costs and tax costs. A Harvard study concludes that the tax component is 22 percent. We are competing in a global economy with a 22 percent tax component in our price system making us less than competitive and driving jobs offshore.

And the lowest income people? You always hear about how sales taxes hurt the lowest income earners: They are currently losing 22 percent of their purchasing power today to the current system.

Any tax bill that nibbles around the edges of the current income tax system—whether it is the flat tax or any other iteration and leaves the IRS in place—doesn't touch any of those things. The FairTax fixes them all.

The FairTax is a single, universal, at-the-retail-checkout sales tax on the purchase of new goods and services. There is no tax on used goods, since nothing should be taxed more than once.

There is no tax on business activity. There is no tax on personal income, corporate income, dividends, estates. There is no gift tax, alternate minimum tax, capital gains tax, dividend tax. All gone— along with the IRS.

Currently average income earners give the federal government 23 cents of every dollar they earn—15 percent income tax and 8 percent being their share of the payroll tax. Under the FairTax you would give the government 23 percent of every dollar you spend. If you don't spend it, you are not taxed on it. All income taxes are gone and you get a $4 trillion, 10-year tax cut by getting rid of the compliance costs. You increase the purchasing power of all Americans, through reductions in price and increases in take-home pay, by 22 percent.

We will become a global powerhouse because we will be selling into a global economy without the tax component in our price system.

When Bill Archer was chairman of the Ways and Means Committee, he used to quote from a study of 500 international corporations. Phone calls had been made to these corporations headquartered in Europe and Japan, and they were asked: What would you do in your long-term planning if the United States government eliminated all taxes on capital and labor and taxed only personal consumption? Eighty percent said they would build their next plant in the United States.

And, in truth, if you are selling to Detroit, you would rather be in Detroit because of transportation costs. But because of the tax component in the price system, we are not in Detroit.

One of the things we learned from the $22 million worth of private research we had done is that the American people want to protect the low-income earners. So we devised a prebate system, which is a rebate at the beginning of the month, not at the end. The government would transfer to every household a distribution sufficient to totally untax them on necessities, based not on income but on the size of the household. And we don't get into the business of defining necessities. I had a friend in Congress who was a supporter of this plan, but he wanted to make sure that we taxed potato chips and not potatoes.

I said that is the boat we are in now—picking winners and losers. So we took the government definition of poverty-level spending: the spending necessary for a given-size household to buy their essentials. A household of four can spend $30,000 with no tax consequences. Beyond that everybody pays the same.

With this approach, we are all voluntary taxpayers. We pay taxes when we choose, as much as we choose, by how we choose to spend.

The FairTax bill has a provision for getting rid of the Sixteenth Amendment. What the language says if we haven't repealed the Sixteenth Amendment after seven years under the FairTax system, all the income taxes come back. After seven years, we believe that the American people will put enough pressure on their members of Congress to encourage them to eliminate the Sixteenth Amendment.

For as long as we have been taxing individuals in this country, we have only taxed wages. We have never taxed wealth. When Warren Buffett complains that his secretary is paying a higher tax rate than he is, it is because she works for wages. The first thing wealthy people do is to stop getting wages. They live on capital gains and dividends that are taxed at a lower rate. And that tax rate is lower because they have already paid a higher rate on that money in corporate income taxes. They are already being taxed twice.

The FairTax taxes *spent wealth* rather than *earned wages*.

This year the federal government is going to collect about $2.3 trillion in income taxes. The FairTax would bring in 10 percent more than that. With politicians running around Washington looking for sources of revenue, they ought to be looking this way.

The United States will turn to the FairTax one day. Not out of a sense that it is the wisest approach, but out of the realization that there is no place else to go. The top two percent cannot continue to pay the whole bill. We keep thinking that you can just raise the tax on those very wealthy people, but there is little money there; the money is in the middle class.

Also, rich people are often pretty smart. Two years ago, when Maryland tried to raise more revenue, they found there were 3,000 ultra-high income earners in the state. They drafted a bill to affect just those few high-income earners. A few months after that bill passed, there were only 1,000 high-income earners in Maryland. And I would be surprised if they haven't all left by now.

The FairTax broadens the base and lowers the tax rate. Everybody is treated exactly the same. Under the FairTax when Warren Buffett's wealth is spent—and it will be spent, if not by him, then by his heirs or by foundations—it will be taxed at exactly the same rate as his secretary's and he will be proud.

The FairTax gives the American people the ultimate gift that freedom has to give—the gift of anonymity. Never should an agency of government know more about us than we are willing to tell our children.

LUDWIG VON MISES

EXCERPTS FROM

HUMAN ACTION

XXVIII. Interference by Taxation

1. The Neutral Tax

To keep the social apparatus of coercion and compulsion running requires expenditure of labor and commodities. Under a liberal system of government these expenditures are small compared with the sum of the individuals' incomes. The more the government expands the sphere of its activities, the more its budget increases.

If the government itself owns and operates plants, farms, forests, and mines, it might consider covering a part or the whole of its financial needs from interest and profit earned. But government operation of business enterprises as a rule is so inefficient that it results in losses rather than in profits. Governments must resort to taxation, i.e., they must raise revenues by forcing the subjects to surrender a part of their wealth or income.

Ludwig von Mises, *Human Action: A Treatise on Economics*, 4th revised edition (San Francisco, CA: Fox & Wilkes, 1996), 737–42, 804–11. See also the Ludwig von Mises Institute—http://mises.org/Books/humanaction.pdf.

A neutral mode of taxation is conceivable that would not divert the operation of the market from the lines in which it would develop in the absence of any taxation. However, the vast literature on problems of taxation as well as the policies of governments have hardly ever given thought to the problem of the *neutral* tax. They have been more eager to find the *just* tax.

The neutral tax would affect the conditions of the citizens only to the extent required by the fact that a part of the labor and material goods available is absorbed by the government apparatus. In the imaginary construction of the evenly rotating economy the treasury continually levies taxes and spends the whole amount raised, neither more nor less, for defraying the costs incurred by the activities of the government's officers. A part of each citizen's income is spent for public expenditure. If we assume that in such an evenly rotating economy there prevails perfect income equality in such a way that every household's income is proportional to the number of its members, both a head tax and a proportional income tax would be neutral taxes. Under these assumptions there would be no difference between them. A part of each citizen's income would be absorbed by public expenditure, and no secondary effects of taxation would emerge.

The changing economy is entirely different from this imaginary construction of an evenly rotating economy with income equality. Continuous change and the inequality of wealth and income are essential and necessary features of the changing market economy, the only real and working system of the market economy. In the frame of such a system no tax can be neutral. The very idea of a neutral tax is as unrealizable as that of neutral money. But of course, the reasons for this inescapable non-neutrality are different in the case of taxes from what they are in the case of money.

A head tax that taxes every citizen equally and uniformly without any regard to the size of his income and wealth, falls more heavily upon those with more moderate means than upon those with more ample means. It restricts the production of the articles consumed by the masses more sharply than that of the articles mainly consumed by the wealthier citizens. On the other hand, it tends to curtail saving and capital accumulation less than a more burdensome taxation of the wealthier citizens does. It does not slow down the tendency toward a drop in the marginal productivity of capital goods as against the marginal productivity of labor to the same extent as does taxation discriminating against those with higher income and wealth, and consequently it does not to the same extent retard the tendency toward a rise in wage rates.

The actual fiscal policies of all countries are today exclusively guided by the idea that taxes should be apportioned according to each citizen's "ability to pay." In the considerations which finally resulted in the general acceptance of the ability-to-pay principle there was some dim conception that taxing the well-to-do more heavily than those with moderate means renders a tax somewhat more neutral. However this may be, it is certain that any reference to tax neutrality was very soon entirely discarded. The ability-to-pay principle has been raised to the dignity of a postulate of social justice. As people see it today, the fiscal and budgetary objectives of taxation are of secondary importance only. The primary function of taxation is to reform social conditions according to justice. From this point of view, a tax appears as the more satisfactory the less neutral it is and the more it serves as a device for diverting production and consumption from those lines into which the unhampered market would have directed them.

2. The Total Tax

The idea of social justice implied in the ability-to-pay principle is that of perfect financial equality of all citizens. As long as any inequality of income of wealth remains it can as plausibly be argued that these larger incomes and fortunes, however small their absolute amount, indicate some excess of ability to be levied upon, as it can be argued that any existing inequalities of income and wealth indicate differences in ability. The only logical stopping place of the ability-to-pay doctrine is at the complete equalization of incomes and wealth by confiscation of all incomes and fortunes above the lowest amount in the hands of anyone.[1]

---

[1] Cf. Harley Lutz, *Guideposts to a Free Economy* (New York, 1945), p. 76.

The notion of the total tax is the antithesis of the notion of the neutral tax. The total tax completely taxes away—confiscates—all incomes and estates. Then the government, out of the community chest thus filled, gives to everybody an allowance for defraying the costs of his sustenance. Or, what comes to the same thing, the government in taxing leaves free that amount which it considers everybody's fair share and completes the shares of those who have less up to the amount of their fair share.

The idea of the total tax cannot be thought out to its ultimate logical consequences. If the entrepreneurs and capitalists do not derive any personal benefit or damage from their utilization of the means of production, they become indifferent with regard to the choice between various modes of conduct. Their social function fades away, and they become disinterested irresponsible administrators of public property. They are no longer bound to adjust production to the wishes of the consumers. If only the income is taxed away while the capital stock itself is left free, an incentive is offered to the owners to consume parts of their wealth and thus to hurt the interests of everyone. A total income tax would be a very inept means for the transformation of capitalism into socialism. If the total tax affects wealth no less than income, it is no longer a tax, i.e., a device for collecting government revenue within a market economy. It becomes a measure for the transition to socialism. As soon as it is consummated, socialism has been substituted for capitalism.

Even when looked upon as a method for the realization of socialism, the total tax is disputable. Some socialists launched plans for a prosocialist tax reform. They recommended either a 100 per cent estate and gift tax or taxing away totally the rent of land or all unearned income—i.e., in the socialist terminology, all revenue not derived from manual labor performed. The examination of these projects is superfluous. It is enough to know that they are utterly incompatible with the preservation of the market economy.

3. Fiscal and Nonfiscal Objectives of Taxation

The fiscal and nonfiscal objectives of taxation do not agree with one another.

Consider, for instance, excise duties on liquor. If one considers them as a source of government revenue, the more they yield the better they appear. Of course, as the duty must enhance the price of the beverage, it restricts sales and consumption. It is necessary to find out by testing under what rate of duty the yield becomes highest. But if one looks at liquor taxes as a means of reducing the consumption of liquor as much as possible, the rate is better the higher it is. Pushed beyond a certain limit, the tax makes consumption drop considerably, and also the revenue concomitantly. If the tax fully attains its nonfiscal objective of weaning people entirely from drinking alcoholic beverages, the revenue is zero. It no longer serves any fiscal purpose: its effects are merely prohibitive. The same is valid not only with regard to all kinds of indirect taxation but no less for direct taxation. Discriminating taxes levied upon corporations and big business would, if raised above a certain limit, result in the total disappearance of corporations and big business. Capital levies, inheritance and estate taxes, and income taxes are similarly self-defeating if carried to extremes.

There is no solution for the irreconcilable conflict between the fiscal and the nonfiscal ends of taxation. The power to tax involves, as Chief Justice Marshall pertinently observed, the power to destroy. This power can be used for the destruction of the market economy, and it is the firm resolution of many governments and parties to use it for this purpose. With the substitution of socialism for capitalism, the dualism of the coexistence of two distinct spheres of action disappears. The government swallows the whole orbit of the individual's autonomous actions and becomes totalitarian. It no longer depends for its financial support on the means exacted from the citizens. There is no longer any such thing as a separation of public funds and private funds.

Taxation is a matter of the market economy. It is one of the characteristic features of the market economy that the government does not interfere with the market phenomena and that its technical apparatus is so small that its maintenance absorbs only a modest fraction of the total sum of the individual citizens' incomes. Then taxes are an appropriate vehicle for providing the funds needed by the government. They are appropriate because they are low and do not perceptibly disarrange production and consumption. If taxes grow beyond a moderate limit, they cease to be taxes and turn into devices for the destruction of the market economy.

The metamorphosis of taxes into weapons of destruction is the mark of present-day public finance. We do not deal with the quite arbitrary value judgments concerning the problems of whether heavy taxation is a curse or a benefit and whether the expenditures financed by the tax yield are or are not wise and beneficial.[2] What matters is that the heavier taxation becomes, the less compatible it is with the preservation of the market economy. There is no need to raise the question of whether or not it is true that "no country was ever ruined by large expenditures of money by the public and for the public."[3] It cannot be denied that the market economy can be ruined by large public expenditures and that it is the intention of many people to ruin it in this way.

Businessmen complain about the oppressiveness of heavy taxes. Statesmen are alarmed about the danger of "eating the seedcorn." Yet, the true crux of the taxation issue is to be seen in the paradox that the more taxes increase, the more they undermine the market economy and concomitantly the system of taxation itself. Thus the fact becomes manifest that ultimately the preservation of private property and confiscatory measures are incompatible. Every specific tax, as well as a nation's whole tax system, becomes self-defeating above a certain height of the rates.

4. The Three Classes of Tax Interventionism

The various methods of taxation which can be used for the regulation of the economy—i.e., as instruments of an interventionist policy—can be classified in three groups:

1. The tax aims at totally suppressing or at restricting the production of definite commodities. It thus indirectly interferes with consumption too. It does not matter whether this end is aimed at by the imposition of special taxes or by exempting certain products from a general

---

[2] This is the customary method of dealing with problems of public finance. Cf., e.g., Ely Adams, Lorenz, and Young, *Outlines of Economics* (3d ed. New York, 1920), p. 702.

[3] Ibid.

tax imposed upon all other products or upon those products which the consumer would have preferred in the absence of fiscal discrimination. Tax exemption is employed as an instrument of interventionism in the case of customs duties. The domestic product is not burdened by the tariff which affects only the merchandise imported from abroad. Many countries resort to tax discrimination in regulating domestic production. They try, for instance, to encourage the production of wine, a product of small or medium-size grape growers, as against the production of beer, a product of big-size breweries, by submitting beer to a more burdensome excise tax than wine.

2. The tax expropriates a part of income or wealth.

3. The tax expropriates income and wealth entirely.

We do not have to deal with the third class, as it is merely a means for the realization of socialism and as such is outside the scope of interventionism. The first class is in its effects not different from the restrictive measures dealt with in the following chapter. The second class encompasses confiscatory measures dealt with in Chapter XXXII.

XXXII. Confiscation and Redistribution

1. The Philosophy of Confiscation

Interventionism is guided by the idea that interfering with property rights does not affect the size of production. The most naive manifestation of this fallacy is presented by confiscatory interventionism. The yield of production activities is considered a given magnitude independent of the merely accidental arrangements of society's social order. The task of the government is seen as the "fair" distribution of this national income among the various members of society.

The interventionists and the socialists contend that all commodities are turned out by a social process of production. When this process comes to an end and its fruits ripen, a second social process, that of distribution of the yield, follows and allots a share to each. The characteristic feature of the capitalist order is that the shares allotted are unequal. Some people—the entrepreneurs, the capitalists, and the landowners—appropriate to themselves more than they should. Accordingly, the portions of other people are curtailed. Government should by rights expropriate the surplus of the privileged and distribute it among the underprivileged.

Now in the market economy this alleged dualism of two independent processes, that of production and that of distribution, does not exist. There is only one process going on. Goods are not first produced and then distributed. There is no such thing as an appropriation of portions out of a stock of ownerless goods. The products come into existence as somebody's property. If one wants to distribute them, one must first confiscate them. It is certainly very easy for the governmental apparatus of compulsion and coercion to embark upon confiscation and expropriation. But this does not prove that a durable system of economic affairs can be built upon such confiscation and expropriation.

When the Vikings turned their backs upon a community of autarkic peasants whom they had plundered, the surviving victims began to work, to till the soil, and to build again. When the pirates returned after some years, they again found things to seize. But capitalism cannot stand such reiterated predatory raids. Its capital accumulation and investments are founded upon the expectation that no such expropriation will occur. If this expectation is absent, people will prefer to consume their capital instead of safeguarding it for the expropriators. This is the inherent error of all plans that aim at combining private ownership and reiterated expropriation.

2. Land Reform

The social reformers of older days aimed at the establishment of a community of autarkic farmers only. The shares of land allotted to each member were to be equal. In the imagination of these utopians there is no room for division of labor and specialization in processing trades. It is a serious mistake to call such a social order *agrarian socialism*. It is merely a juxtaposition of economically self-sufficient households.

In the market economy the soil is a means of production like any other material factor of production. Plans aiming at a more or less equal distribution of the soil among the farming population are, under the conditions of the market economy, merely plans for granting privileges to a group of less efficient producers at the expense of the immense majority of consumers. The operation of the market tends to eliminate all those farmers whose cost of production is higher than the marginal costs needed for the production of that amount of farm products the consumers are ready to buy. It determines the size of the farms as well as the methods of production applied. If the government interferes in order to make a different arrangement of the conditions of farming prevail, it raises the average price of farm products. If under competitive conditions *m* farmers, each of them operating a 1,000-acre farm, produce all those farm products the consumers are ready to acquire, and the government interferes in order to substitute 5 *m* farmers, each of them operating a 200-acre farm, for *m*, the previous numbers of farmers, the consumers foot the bill.

It is vain to justify such land reforms by referring to natural law and other metaphysical ideas. The simple truth is that they enhance the price of agricultural products and that they also impair nonagricultural production. As more manpower is needed to turn out a unit of farm produce, more people are employed in farming and less are left for the processing industries. The total amount of commodities available for consumption drops and a certain group of people is favored at the expense of the majority.

3. Confiscatory Taxation

Today the main instrument of confiscatory interventionism is taxation. It does not matter whether the objective of estate and income taxation is the allegedly social motive of equalizing wealth and income or whether the primary motive is that of revenue. What alone counts is the resulting effect.

The average man looks at the problems involved with unveiled envy. Why should anybody be richer than he himself is? The lofty moralist conceals his resentment in philosophical disquisitions. He argues that a man who owns ten millions cannot be made happier by an increment of ninety millions more. Inversely, a man who owns a hundred millions does not feel any impairment of happiness if his wealth is reduced to a bare ten millions only. The same reasoning holds good for excessive incomes.

To judge in this way means to judge from an individualistic point of view. The yardstick applied is the supposed sentiments of individuals. Yet the problems involved are social problems; they must be appraised with regard to their social consequences. What matters is neither the happiness of any Croesus nor his personal merits or demerits; it is society and the productivity of human effort.

A law that prohibits any individual from accumulating more than ten millions or from making more than one million a year restricts the activities of precisely those entrepreneurs who are most successful in filing the wants of consumers. If such a law had been enacted in the United States fifty years ago, many who are multimillionaires today would live in more modest circumstances. But all those new branches of industry which supply the masses with articles unheard of before would operate, if at all, on a much smaller scale, and their products would be beyond the reach of the common man. It is manifestly contrary to the interest of the consumers to prevent the most efficient entrepreneurs from expanding the sphere of their activities up to the limit to which the public approves of their conduct of business by buying their products. Here again the issue is who should be supreme, the consumers or the government? In the unhampered market the behavior of consumers, their buying or abstention from buying, ultimately determines each individual's income and wealth. Should one vest in the government the power to overrule the consumers' choices?

The incorrigible statolatrist objects. In his opinion what motivates the activities of the great entrepreneur is not the lust for wealth, but the lust for power. Such a "royal merchant" would not restrict his activities if he had to deliver all the surplus earned to the tax collector. His lust for power cannot be weakened by any considerations of mere moneymaking. Let us, for the sake of argument, accept this psychology. But on what else is the power of a businessman founded than on his wealth? How would Rockefeller and Ford have been in a position to acquire "power" if they had been prevented from acquiring wealth? After all, those statolatrists are on comparatively better grounds who want to prohibit the accumulation of wealth precisely because it gives a man economic power.[1]

Taxes are necessary. But the system of discriminatory taxation universally accepted under the misleading name of progressive taxation of income and inheritance is not a mode of taxation. It is rather a mode of disguised expropriation of the successful capitalists and entrepreneurs. Whatever the governments' satellites may advance in its favor, it is incompatible with the preservation of the market economy. It can at best be considered a means of bringing about socialism. Looking backward on the evolution of income tax rates from the beginning of the Federal income tax in 1913 until the present day, one can hardly believe that the tax will not soon absorb 100 per cent of all the surplus above the average height of the common man's wages.

Economics is not concerned with the spurious metaphysical doctrines advanced in favor of tax progression, but with its repercussions on the operation of the market economy. The interventionist authors and politicians look at the problems involved from the angle of their arbitrary notions of what is "socially desirable." As they see it, "the purpose of taxation is never to raise money," since the government "can raise all the money it needs by printing it." The true purpose of taxation is "to leave less in the hands of the taxpayer."[2]

Economists approach the issue from a different angle. They ask first: what are the effects of confiscatory taxation on capital accumulation? The greater part of that portion of the higher incomes which is taxed away would have been used for the accumulation of additional capital. If the treasury employs the proceeds for current expenditure, the result is a drop in the amount of capital accumulation. The same is valid, even to a greater extent, for death taxes. They force the heirs to sell a considerable part of the testator's estate. This capital is, of course, not destroyed; it merely changes ownership. But the savings of the purchasers, which are spent for the acquisition of the capital sold by the heirs, would have constituted a net increment in capital available.

---

[1] There is no need to emphasize again that the use of the terminology of political rule is entirely inadequate in the treatment of economic problems.

[2] Cf. A. B. Lerner, *The Economics of Control, Principles of Welfare Economics* (New York, 1944), pp. 308–308.

Thus the accumulation of new capital is slowed down. The realization of technological improvement is impaired; the quota of capital invested per worker employed is reduced; a check is placed upon the rise in the marginal productivity of labor and upon the concomitant rise in real wage rates. It is obvious that the popular belief that this mode of confiscatory taxation harms only the immediate victims, the rich, is false.

If capitalists are faced with the likelihood that the income tax or the estate tax will rise to 100 per cent, they will prefer to consume their capital funds rather than to preserve them for the tax collector.

Confiscatory taxation results in checking economic progress and improvement not only by its effect upon capital accumulation. It brings about a general trend toward stagnation and the preservation of business practices which could not last under the competitive conditions of the unhampered market economy.

It is an inherent feature of capitalism that it is no respecter of vested interests and forces every capitalist and entrepreneur to adjust his conduct of business anew each day to the changing structure of the market. Capitalists and entrepreneurs are never free to relax. As long as they remain in business they are never granted the privilege of quietly enjoying the fruits of their ancestors' and their own achievements and of lapsing into a routine. If they forget that their task is to serve the consumers to the best of their abilities, they will very soon forfeit their eminent position and will be thrown back into the ranks of the common man. Their leadership and their funds are continually challenged by newcomers.

Every ingenious man is free to start new business projects. He may be poor, his funds may be modest and most of them may be borrowed. But if he fills the wants of consumers in the best and cheapest way, he will succeed by means of "excessive" profits. He ploughs back the greater part of his profits into his business, thus making it grow rapidly. It is the activity of such enterprising parvenus that provides the market economy with its "dynamism." These nouveaux riches are the harbingers of economic improvement. Their threatening competition forces the old firms and big corporations either to adjust their conduct to the best possible service of the public or to go out of business.

But today taxes often absorb the greater part of the newcomer's "excessive" profits. He cannot accumulate capital; he cannot expand his own business; he will never become big business and a match for the vested interests. The old firms do not need to fear his competition; they are sheltered by the tax collector. They may with impunity indulge in routine, they may defy the wishes of the public and become conservative. It is true, the income tax prevents them, too, from accumulating new capital. But what is more important for them is that it prevents the dangerous newcomer from accumulating any capital. They are virtually privileged by the tax system. In this sense progressive taxation checks economic progress and makes for rigidity. While under unhampered capitalism the ownership of capital is a liability forcing the owner to serve the consumers, modern methods of taxation transform it into a privilege.

The interventionists complain that big business is getting rigid and bureaucratic and that it is no longer possible for competent newcomers to challenge the vested interests of the old rich families. However, as far as their complaints are justified, they complain about things which are merely the result of their own policies.

Profits are the driving force of the market economy. The greater the profits, the better the needs of the consumers are supplied. For profits can only be reaped by removing discrepancies between the demands of the consumers and the previous state of production activities. He who serves the public best, makes the highest profits. In fighting profits governments deliberately sabotage the operation of the market economy.

Confiscatory Taxation and Risk-Taking

A popular fallacy considers entrepreneurial profit a reward for risk-taking. It looks upon the entrepreneur as a gambler who invests in a lottery after having weighed the favorable chances of winning a prize against the unfavorable chances of losing his stake. This opinion manifests itself most clearly in the description of stock-exchange transactions as a sort of gambling. From the point of view of this widespread fable, the evil caused by confiscatory taxation is that it disarranges the ratio between the favorable and the unfavorable chances in the lottery. The prizes are cut down, while the unfavorable hazards remain unchanged. Thus capitalists and entrepreneurs are discouraged from embarking upon risky ventures.

Every word in this reasoning is false. The owner of capital does not choose between more risky, less risky, and safe investments. He is forced by the very operation of the market economy, to invest his funds in such a way as to supply the most urgent needs of the consumers to the best possible extent. If the methods of taxation resorted to by the government bring about capital consumption or restrict the accumulation of new capital, the capital required for marginal employments is lacking and an expansion of investment which would have been effected in the absence of these taxes is prevented. The wants of the consumers are satisfied to a lesser extent only. But this outcome is not caused by a reluctance of capitalists to take risks; it is caused by a drop in capital supply.

There is no such thing as a safe investment. If capitalists were to behave in the way the risk fable describes and were to strive after what they consider to be the safest investment, their conduct would render this line of investment unsafe and they would certainly lose their input. For the capitalist there is no means of evading the law of the market that makes it imperative for the investor to comply with the wishes of the consumers and to produce all that can be produced under the given state of capital supply, technological knowledge, and the valuations of the consumers. A capitalist never chooses that investment in which, according to his understanding of the future, the danger of losing his input is smallest. He chooses that investment in which he expects to make the highest possible profit.

Those capitalists who are aware of their own lack of ability to judge correctly for themselves the trend of the market do not invest in equity capital, but lend their funds to the owners of such venture capital. They thus enter into a sort of partnership with those on whose better ability to appraise the conditions of the market they rely. It is customary to call venture capital *risk* capital. However, as has been pointed out, the success or failure of the investment in preferred stock, bonds, debentures, mortgages, and other loans depends ultimately also on the same factors that determine success or failure of the venture capital invested.[3] There is no such thing as independence of the vicissitudes of the market.

If taxation were to strengthen the supply of loan capital at the expense of the supply of venture capital, it would make the gross market rate of interest drop and at the same time, by increasing the share of borrowed capital as against the share of equity capital in the capital structure of the firms and corporations, render the investment in loans more uncertain. The process would therefore be self-liquidating.

The fact that a capitalist as a rule does not concentrate his investments, both in common stock and in loans, in one enterprise or one branch of business, but prefers to spread out his funds among various classes of investment does not suggest that he wants to reduce his "gambling risk." He wants to improve his chances of earning profits.

Nobody embarks upon any investment if he does not expect to make a good investment. Nobody deliberately chooses a malinvestment. It is only the emergence of conditions not properly anticipated by the investor that turns an investment into a malinvestment.

As has been pointed out, there cannot be such a thing as non-invested capital.[4] The capitalist is not free to choose between investment and noninvestment. Neither is he free to deviate in the choice of his investments in capital goods from the lines determined by the most urgent among the still-unsatisfied wants of the consumers. He must try to anticipate these future wants correctly. Taxes may reduce the amount of capital goods available by bring about consumption of capital. But they do not restrict the employment of all capital goods available.[5]

With an excessive height of the income and estate tax rules for the very rich, a capitalist may consider it the most advisable thing to keep all his funds in cash or in bank balances not bearing any interest. He consumes part of his capital, pays no income tax and reduces the inheritance tax which his heirs will have to pay. But even if people really behave this way, their conduct does not affect the employment of the capital available. It affects prices. But no capital good remains

---

[3] Cf. above, pp. 539–540.
[4] Cf. above, pp. 521–523.
[5] In using the term "capital goods available," due consideration should be given to the problem of convertibility.

uninvested on account of it. And the operation of the market pushes investment into those lines in which it is expected to satisfy the most urgent not yet satisfied demand of the buying public.